Graph Neural Network-Based Detection and Attribution of Advanced Persistent Threats

Shon Kon

Table of Contents

1 Introduction

Advanced Persistent Threats (APTs) are regarded as one of the most sophisticated categories of cyberattacks, frequently associated with well-resourced or state-sponsored adversaries. Unlike conventional intrusions that are often opportunistic and short-lived, APTs are characterized by their ability to remain hidden within a target environment for extended periods while maintaining continuous access. This persistence and stealth significantly increase the risks they pose to governments, enterprises, and critical infrastructures [27, 6].

What distinguishes APT operations is the scale and duration of their campaigns, which may extend over months or even years. These adversaries employ a wide range of techniques to infiltrate networks, sustain their presence, and pursue objectives such as espionage, information theft, or operational disruption [28, 29, 30]. Their ability to conceal malicious actions within normal system behavior enables them to bypass traditional detection solutions, making them particularly difficult to counter [29, 31, 32]. As a result, effective defense requires continuous monitoring, long-term correlation of activities, and methods capable of uncovering subtle, coordinated malicious patterns.

The attack lifecycle of an APT typically unfolds across multiple stages. Initial access is often obtained through social engineering, software vulnerability exploitation, or insider threats [33, 28]. Once inside, adversaries establish persistence and gather intelligence about the target environment, which informs their subsequent actions [29, 31]. They then perform lateral movement and privilege escalation to compromise more valuable assets and extend their control within the network [30, 32]. The final stage generally involves the execution of the adversary's goals, such as exfiltrating sensitive data, implanting additional malware, or maintaining long-term covert access, while actively employing evasion techniques to remain undetected [33, 28, 29]. The adaptive, multi-step nature of these operations highlights the need for detection models that can capture broader behavioral contexts, rather than relying solely on short-term anomalies.

System audit logs are an invaluable resource for identifying such attacks, as they provide detailed traces of activity across the operating system. When these logs are modeled as provenance graphs, they provide a structured representation of system entities, including processes, files, registry keys, scheduled tasks, and network connections, along with the relationships between them. In contrast to event-based analysis, which often examines logs in isolation, provenance graphs retain both causality and contextual information, enabling the reconstruction of complex attack chains. However, prior research typically reduces these graphs to only a handful of node and edge types, resulting in significant information loss and limiting their effectiveness in detecting sophisticated adversaries [17, 34, 6].

To address these challenges, this thesis introduces a multi-stage framework that integrates node representation learning, malicious node detection, malicious subgraph construction, and APT attribution into a unified pipeline. The approach leverages graph neural networks tailored to heterogeneous provenance data, supported by residual connections, balanced sampling, and regularization strategies. By combining fine-grained node-level detection with campaign-level attribution, the framework achieves both scalability to large provenance graphs and robustness to class imbalance, while also enhancing interpretability through an attention mechanism. This design provides a principled and efficient way to detect malicious activity and attribute it to specific APT groups.

1.1 Problem Statement

Despite ongoing advances, detecting APTs remains a complex and unresolved challenge. Traditional **rule-based** detection methods rely on predefined signatures or handcrafted rules, which adversaries can easily bypass by modifying or slightly altering their techniques. Such methods are often effective only against already known threats and are incapable of adapting to new or evolving attack strategies [29, 31, 32].

Anomaly detection models have been introduced as a more adaptive alternative, aiming to flag deviations from regular activity. However, these approaches frequently generate excessive false positives, since not all unusual system behavior is malicious. In practice, this overloads analysts and undermines the system's usability [28, 30]. Moreover, many anomaly detection systems fail to learn from adversarial behaviors over time, leaving them unable to keep pace with evolving threats [33].

Provenance graph–based methods provide a promising path forward because they capture interactions among system entities and preserve the causal structure of events [17, 34]. This enables a more comprehensive analysis of coordinated, multi-stage campaigns. Yet, existing studies often simplify provenance graphs to include only processes and files, omitting other critical entities such as registry keys, scheduled tasks, DLLs, or named pipes [6]. These omissions can obscure subtle yet significant behaviors leveraged by attackers to evade detection and maintain persistence. Conversely, the inclusion of all such entities also raises scalability challenges due to the rapid growth and complexity of the resulting graphs.

Furthermore, most existing APT detection techniques are limited to identifying suspicious events or anomalies without reconstructing the whole attack chain or associating it with a specific APT group [28, 29]. While this may provide initial alerts, it does not supply defenders with the broader intelligence required to understand the adversary's intent, origin, or likely future actions. Without attribution, the practical value of detection remains limited, as security teams cannot tailor their responses to specific threat actors [31, 32]. These challenges underscore the necessity of a holistic approach that integrates detailed provenance analysis with both detection and attribution.

1.2 Research Objectives

The main objectives of this research are:

- To develop a method for constructing heterogeneous provenance graphs from system audit logs, preserving a wide range of entities (processes, files, registry keys, DLLs, scheduled tasks, etc.) and their interactions.
- To design a GNN-based detection model that integrates GraphSAGE and GAT layers with edge attributes, enabling node-level classification that leverages both neighbor importance and relation types for accurate malicious entity detection.
- To perform malicious subgraph extraction that expands around detected nodes and incorporates bridge structures, ensuring sufficient attack context for downstream classification.
- To apply multi-class classification on the extracted subgraphs for attributing attacks to specific APT groups, providing actionable threat intelligence beyond simple detection.

- To validate the complete framework using a controlled dataset of simulated APT campaigns spanning multiple groups and attack days, reflecting realistic multi-stage adversarial strategies.

1.3 Contributions

The contributions of this thesis can be summarized as follows:

- A comprehensive, up-to-date dataset of simulated APT campaigns, that includes diverse and recently observed attack scenarios, realistic adversarial tactics, and attacks targeting modern operating systems, particularly Windows-based infrastructures. The dataset will reflect realistic adversary behaviors and support reproducible evaluation.
- A graph construction method that generates heterogeneous provenance graphs from raw audit logs, capturing a broader set of entities and relations than prior works and preserving the causal structure for analysis.
- A GNN-based detection framework that combines GraphSAGE and GAT layers with edge attributes for binary node classification. This design addresses class imbalance and mitigates oversmoothing while highlighting the importance of both neighbor nodes and relation types.
- An attribution module that extracts semantically rich malicious subgraphs and classifies them into known APT groups. This represents the most significant novelty of the research, as it moves beyond detection toward actionable attribution, offering more profound insights into adversary identity and methodology, which is overlooked by prior works.

Overall, this research aims to bridge the gap between theoretical approaches to APT detection and practical implementation by providing a scalable, graph-based framework that supports both fine-grained detection of malicious entities and campaign-level attribution. The subsequent sections of this proposal will present related work, the proposed methodology, dataset construction, and evaluation strategies in detail.

2 Literature Review

2.1 Overview of Advanced Persistent Threats

Advanced Persistent Threats (APTs) are among the most organized and enduring forms of cyberattacks. First introduced by the United States Air Force (USAF) in 2006 as a term to discuss cyber intrusions without disclosing classified intelligence [35], APTs differ fundamentally from conventional cyber threats. Whereas traditional attacks often rely on large-scale, opportunistic exploitation, APTs are highly targeted, typically directed against government agencies, financial institutions, defense contractors, and other high-value organizations. Their defining characteristics include stealth, persistence, and the ability to evade traditional defenses while maintaining long-term access to compromised systems [36]. Attackers frequently rely on spear-phishing, exploitation of zero-day vulnerabilities, and lateral movement across networks to expand their reach and achieve their objectives.

APTs are not opportunistic in nature but rather motivated by strategic goals. These may include long-term espionage, theft of intellectual property, political or military advantage, disruption of critical infrastructure, or financial gain. Unlike cybercriminal groups that prioritize quick profits, APT actors invest significant time and resources in designing, executing, and concealing complex campaigns. This calculated approach enables them to achieve strategic objectives while remaining undetected for extended periods.

The MITRE ATT&CK framework [37] provides a structured view of how APT operations unfold, organizing adversary behavior into a set of tactics that describe "what" an attacker is trying to achieve at each stage. These tactics, while not always executed sequentially, represent the building blocks of an APT campaign:

- **Reconnaissance**: Gathering information on the target environment through scanning, OSINT, or profiling.
- **Resource Development**: Acquiring infrastructure, malware, or accounts used in later stages.
- **Initial Access**: Gaining entry via spear-phishing, exploitation of vulnerabilities, or supply-chain compromise.
- **Execution**: Running malicious code, scripts, or leveraging legitimate tools ("living-off-the-land").
- **Persistence**: Establishing mechanisms such as scheduled tasks or services to maintain long-term access.
- **Privilege Escalation**: Obtaining higher-level permissions to expand influence across the system.
- **Defense Evasion**: Obfuscating code, disabling security tools, or blending into normal user activity.
- **Credential Access**: Stealing or harvesting account credentials through dumping, brute force, or keylogging.
- **Discovery**: Mapping the environment to identify systems, defenses, and potential targets.
- **Lateral Movement**: Pivoting across hosts and domains to compromise additional systems.

- **Collection**: Gathering documents, records, and other data relevant to the mission.
- **Command and Control**: Establishing communication channels to receive commands and exfiltrate data.
- **Exfiltration**: Transferring stolen information out of the network, often encrypted or staged.
- **Impact**: Disrupting or destroying systems and data, e.g., through ransomware or destructive malware.

Although these tactics suggest a progression, APT actors may loop back, skip, or reorder them depending on their objectives and the defenses encountered. This structured representation is valuable both for studying real-world campaigns and for designing detection models that align with adversarial behavior.
Real-world cases, such as APT28 (Fancy Bear), APT29 (Cozy Bear), and the Lazarus Group illustrate the persistence and adaptability of these operations. These groups have demonstrated the ability to tailor their tactics, techniques, and procedures (TTPs) to specific environments, highlighting the critical role of frameworks like MITRE ATT&CK in analyzing, detecting, and defending against APTs.

2.2 Evolution of APT Detection Research

Early research into APTs identified the challenges associated with their detection due to their low-and-slow approach, which allows attackers to blend into regular network activity. The traditional cybersecurity paradigm, which relied heavily on signature-based antivirus and intrusion detection systems (IDS), proved largely ineffective against APTs due to their evolving tactics. This led researchers to explore alternative approaches, including behavioral analysis, anomaly detection, and multi-source data fusion.
Research on APT detection can be categorized into several domains, including network-based, host-based, semantic, and multi-source techniques [38]. Network-based approaches primarily relied on intrusion detection systems (IDS) and network flow analysis. Traditional IDS solutions such as Snort were widely used but were limited to detecting known attack signatures [39]. To address this limitation, researchers explored anomaly-based detection methods that analyzed deviations in network traffic patterns to identify malicious activity. For example, flow-based intrusion detection methods aimed to detect unusual communication patterns associated with command-and-control (C2) traffic and data exfiltration. However, these approaches suffered from high false-positive rates due to legitimate variations in network traffic [40] and do not account for malicious activities conducted locally on the host that do not involve C2 communication, such as privilege escalation, persistence mechanisms, or lateral movement within the system.
Host-based detection methods focused on monitoring system-level events to identify suspicious behavior. Early research in this domain focused on file integrity monitoring (FIM) solutions, which detect unauthorized modifications to critical system files. However, attackers adapted by employing fileless malware techniques, rendering traditional FIM approaches ineffective. Other host-based methods involved kernel-level monitoring and memory analysis to track system calls and process execution patterns. While these techniques provided granular visibility into system activity, they introduced significant performance overheads and required extensive manual analysis [41].

Semantic-based detection approaches aimed to incorporate contextual understanding into APT detection. Researchers developed ontology-based models that mapped attack behaviors to predefined threat patterns [42]. These models leveraged structured knowledge bases to identify indicators of compromise (IOCs) and correlate them with observed system events. While promising, semantic-based detection techniques faced challenges in scalability and adaptability, as attackers constantly evolved their tactics to evade predefined detection rules.

Multi-source domain analysis emerged as a critical approach to APT detection, leveraging data from various security sources, including host logs, network traffic, and application logs. The introduction of Security Information and Event Management (SIEM) systems enabled automated correlation of disparate data sources to identify potential APT activity [43]. However, early SIEM implementations were limited by their reliance on static correlation rules, which often failed to detect novel attack techniques. Researchers proposed log analysis techniques incorporating machine learning and statistical modeling to identify anomalies indicative of APT behavior. These methods aimed to reduce false positives by establishing baselines of regular activity and flagging deviations. However, computational complexity remained challenging, as analyzing large-scale log data in real-time required significant processing power.

One of the most significant advancements in Advanced Persistent Threat (APT) detection has been the introduction of provenance graphs for attack analysis. While defenders often rely on tabular formats for assets like logs, alerts, and firewall rules, attackers leverage a graph-based mindset [3]. Provenance-based detection techniques reconstruct system activity over time, visually representing attack sequences. This methodology lets security analysts track an attacker's movement across a compromised system, correlating multiple low-level events into a coherent attack narrative. Provenance graphs serve as a robust tool for capturing the relationships between various system activities, which can be crucial for identifying malicious actions that may otherwise go undetected by traditional security measures [44, 45, 46].

Early implementations of provenance-based detection systems encountered scalability issues due to the vast volume of system events that required processing [47]. However, these initial challenges laid the groundwork for future graph-based APT detection and attribution of attacks. Recent advancements have focused on enhancing the efficiency of these systems, allowing for real-time analysis and detection of APTs [12, 48]. For instance, systems like HOLMES and UNICORN leverage provenance data to provide timely insights into potential threats, demonstrating the evolution of these techniques from offline investigation tools to dynamic, real-time detection mechanisms [12, 48]. Furthermore, integrating machine learning techniques with provenance graphs has shown promise in improving detection capabilities, enabling the identification of zero-day attacks and other sophisticated threats [49]. The development of provenance graphs has significantly advanced the field of APT detection by providing a structured approach to analyzing complex attack patterns. While scalability remains a concern, ongoing research continues to refine these methods, enhancing their applicability and effectiveness in real-world scenarios [45, 50].

Overall, research on APT detection highlighted several key challenges, including the limitations of signature-based defenses, the high false-positive rates associated with anomaly detection, and the computational overhead of real-time multi-source analysis. Despite these challenges, significant progress was made in developing frameworks that combined network, host, and semantic data sources to improve detection accuracy. The transition towards graph-based and AI-driven analytics in later years built upon the foundations established during this period, paving the way for more effective APT detection mechanisms.

This section reviews relevant studies on APT detection, focusing on existing Machine Learning-based analysis and graph-based APT detection models. A general taxonomy of the Existing work is brought in the subsequent sections and illustrated in Figure 1. This taxonomy provides a structured categorization of log-based APT detection methodologies, integrating machine learning, provenance graph analysis, and hybrid approaches for enhanced detection capabilities.

2.3 Previous Work

In this section, we review prior research relevant to the detection and attribution of advanced persistent threats (APTs). The discussion is organized into two main directions: approaches that do not rely on provenance graphs, and those that leverage provenance information to capture rich system-level interactions. The first group includes methods based on anomaly detection, statistical or learning-based analysis, and domain adaptation of system logs. The second group emphasizes the construction and analysis of provenance graphs, where heterogeneous entities and relationships are modeled to support robust APT detection. By structuring the review in this way, we highlight both the evolution of detection techniques and the advantages and limitations of each line of work, setting the stage for our proposed model.

2.3.1 Non-Provenance graph-based

Coulter et al. [1] propose a domain adaptation-based APT detection method to overcome two major challenges in APT research: the scarcity of representative threat data and the limited generalization of temporal log-based models. They introduce a hybrid adaptation approach, combining *transductive* and *inductive transfer learning*, that projects APT file system interaction patterns (captured from logs) onto a shared representation space using **geodesics distance within a Riemannian manifold**. They further introduce a structured probabilistic model, the **APT Bayesian Network (APT-BN)**, which encodes directory access patterns, file types, extensions, and operations to capture systemic behavioral footprints of malware across campaigns.

The authors utilize three datasets: (1) *APT-EXE*: 9376 known APT logs used for training; (2) WIN_{APT}: 183 real-world APT samples executed on a Windows domain, resulting in 207 logged processes used for testing; and (3) WIN_{Good}: benign Windows processes for both training and testing. As shown in Fig. 2, the architecture supports three analysis pipelines: TFidf, embedding-based models (e.g., Log2Vec), and the proposed domain adaptation method. The adaptation aligns unseen logs with known APT footprints and applies supervised classifiers (e.g., SVM, RF) for detection. Evaluation results demonstrate that the proposed method significantly reduces false positives (under 100 per 100,000 processes) while achieving high behavioral similarity detection, even when trained only on pre-2018 APT logs. The approach outperforms all baselines in F1 score, generalization across campaigns, and stability across temporal domains.

The framework is particularly valuable due to its low FPR, adaptability to unseen log patterns, and its capacity to unify multiple sources into a cohesive detection strategy. Future work includes deeper abstraction of interaction types, adaptive parameter tuning, and inclusion of network behavior logs to complement the file system analysis.

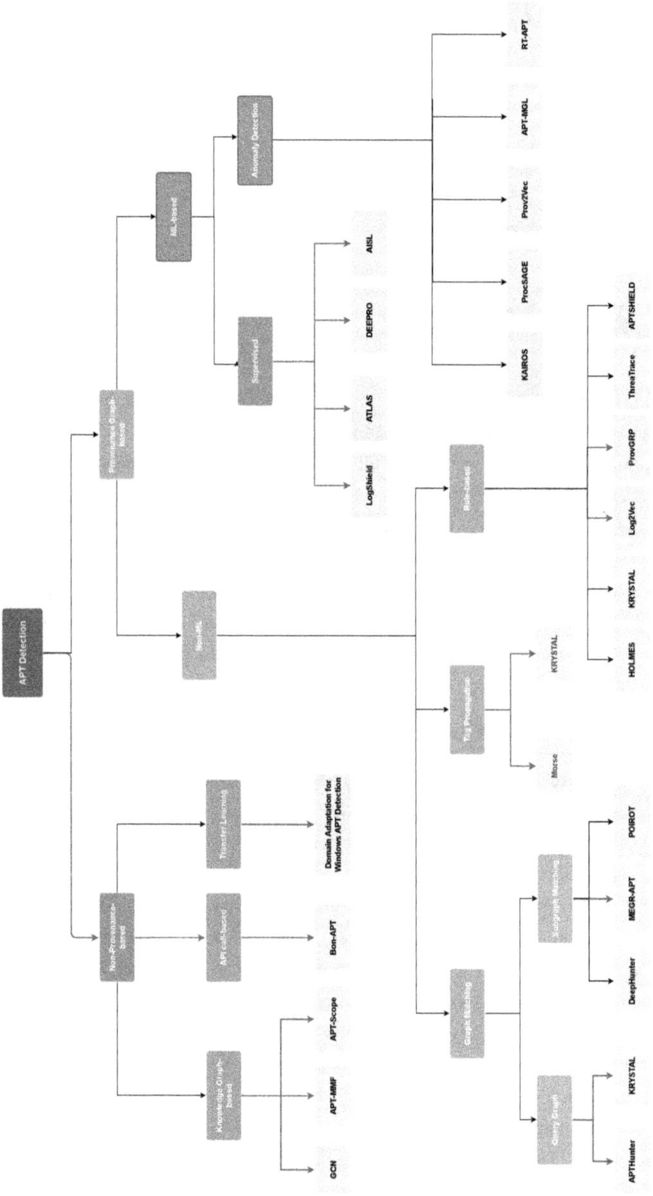

Figure 1: APT Detection Taxonomy

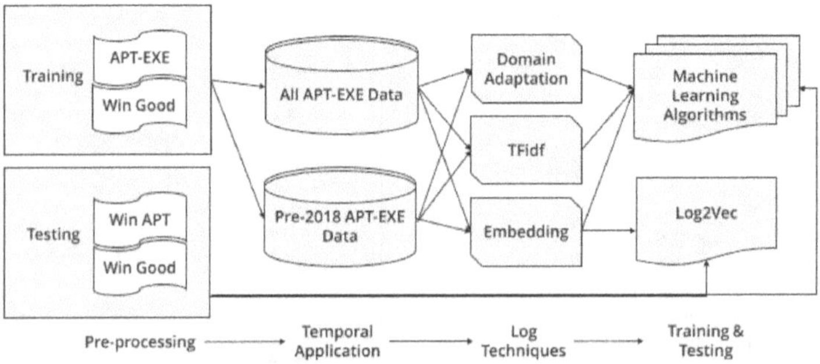

Figure 2: Overview of the APT domain adaptation framework: training/testing datasets, log representation techniques (TFidf, embeddings, domain adaptation), and classifier integration [1].

Shenderovitz and Nissim [2] present **Bon-APT**, a novel temporal learning framework for detecting, attributing, and explaining Advanced Persistent Threats (APTs) based on temporal segmentation of API calls. The system analyzes the dynamic behavior of executable PE files executed in a Cuckoo Sandbox running Windows 10 with full internet access, capturing 270 distinct API calls. These sequences are modeled as multivariate time series data (MTSD) and then segmented over time to capture discrete behavioral phases. As illustrated in Fig. 3, temporal segmentation aggregates API activity across defined segments, enabling the generation of high-level behavioral summaries and reducing noise. Bon-APT abstracts API calls into ten behavioral categories (e.g., file, registry, network operations), which are then used to train Random Forest, LSTM, and multilayer perceptron (MLP) models for detection and attribution. A key strength is its explainability: each segment maps to an interpretable behavioral profile across time.

Bon-APT outperforms state-of-the-art methods across three core tasks: APT detection, group-level attribution, and nation-level attribution, and facilitates a visual comparison of behavior between threat actors. It is evaluated on a large-scale dataset of 121,513 PE samples, including 12,655 APT-labeled files attributed to 188 threat groups and 17 nations. The approach generalizes well across diverse APT strategies while maintaining transparency in its predictions. Limitations include the potential loss of low-level behavioral patterns during segmentation; however, this trade-off significantly enhances noise reduction and interpretability. Future work includes applying deep temporal learning to both abstracted and fine-grained behaviors, and filtering out routine, non-informative activities, such as unpacking, to focus on core attack traits.

Akar and Selvi [3] propose **APT-Scope**, a multistage framework for predicting Advanced Persistent Threat (APT) groups by constructing and analyzing a continuously updated *Heterogeneous Information Network* (HIN) enriched with Cyber Threat Intelligence (CTI) from real-world OSINT data. The architecture consists of three main stages (see Fig. 4): (1) *Data gathering and HIN construction*, which involves extracting IoCs and entities from APT reports using regular expressions and named entity recognition (NER) via SpaCy; (2) *Passive enrichment*, incorporating validated third-party blocklists; and (3) *Active enrichment*, which includes DNS and Whois lookups, SSL queries, port scanning, and social media scraping (e.g., Twitter/X). This comprehensive enrichment pipeline enables the generation of a detailed CTI landscape in the form

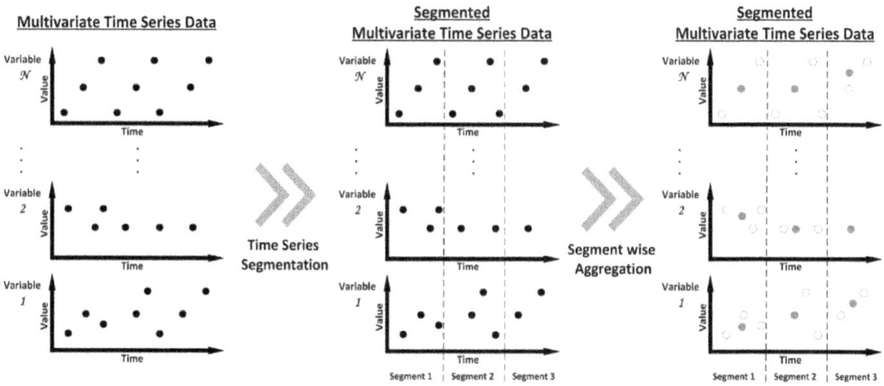

Figure 3: The temporal segmentation process in Bon-APT: multivariate time series data is split and aggregated into behaviorally interpretable segments [2].

of a high-quality HIN composed of millions of nodes and heterogeneous relationships such as inclusion, resolution, and aliasing.

For analysis, APT-Scope applies *FastRP* (Fast Random Projection) for node embedding and *Logistic Regression* to predict missing or new relationships between entities, including alias discovery for APT groups and identification of threat actors behind unknown campaigns (see Fig. 5). The model pipeline includes graph projection, node and link feature engineering, and predictive modeling over mutated HINs. The authors curated 783 APT reports (740 PDF, 43 HTML) and malware datasets from security vendors such as AhnLab, CrowdStrike, ESET, and Check Point, selecting 30% as expert-validated ground truth. They constructed IoC triples and identified meta-paths and meta-graphs across the HIN, enabling rich semantic querying and similarity-based inference.

Evaluation shows that APT-Scope effectively predicts APT group aliases and uncovers threat actors even when direct attribution is missing. The integration of active CTI enrichment and scalable graph-based modeling enables the delivery of high-quality, up-to-date intelligence with actionable insights. Strengths of the system include continuous data collection, relationship prediction from real-world OSINT, and rich structural analysis using meta-graphs. In future work, the authors plan to incorporate additional node types (e.g., operating systems, technology stacks, affected countries), develop a custom APT-aware NER model, and use the HIN for attack forecasting and the discovery of abused services and technologies.

Traditional APT detection methods often struggle to extract the long-term relationships characteristic of multi-stage APT campaigns. To address this, Wang et al. [4] propose a model that leverages Graph Convolutional Networks (GCNs) for APT attack detection, with a specific focus on identifying known attacks through vulnerability and context relationships. The approach comprises three primary stages (see Fig. 6): (1) collecting and organizing data from APT threat intelligence, CVE, CWE, and CAPEC sources to construct a knowledge graph encapsulating APT organizations, vulnerabilities, weaknesses, attack patterns, and methods; (2) transforming this heterogeneous knowledge graph into a homogeneous graph for efficient in-

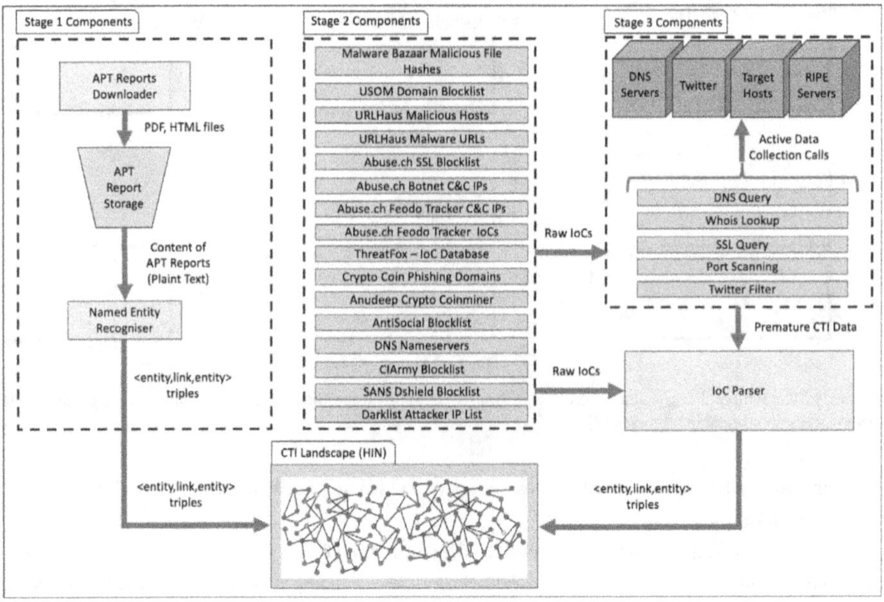

Figure 4: Overview of APT-Scope framework: HIN generation from APT reports and CTI enrichment using passive and active data sources [3].

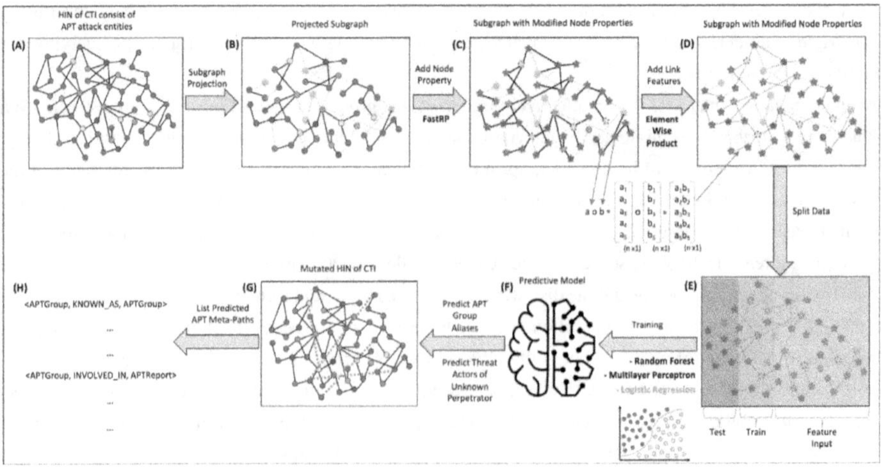

Figure 5: Graph-based machine learning pipeline in APT-Scope: embedding and predictive modeling using FastRP and Logistic Regression [3].

put to the GCN, followed by feature extraction (especially on CVE nodes, using a bag-of-words model and vocabulary-building from preprocessed text); and (3) applying a GCN to the resulting graph structure to propagate and aggregate information across nodes and edges for attack detection. The architecture is designed to represent the knowledge graph as node feature and adjacency matrices, with ReLU activation for feature propagation and a softmax layer for final classification.

During preprocessing, CVE descriptions are cleaned (removing punctuation, stop words, and case sensitivity), tokenized, and converted into feature vectors. Relationships and dependencies between entities (CVE, CWE, CAPEC, attack techniques) are explicitly modeled. The GCN learns to distinguish between benign and APT-related nodes by leveraging these relationships. Evaluation is performed on data targeting 12 APT organizations, utilizing intelligence from sources such as CVE, NVD, CNNVD, Qihoo 360, FireEye, and others. The dataset includes 2435 labeled attack data points and 215 entity relationships, drawn from 1350 APT intelligence reports.

While the approach is promising, it faces certain limitations. Simplifying the heterogeneous graph into a homogeneous form can result in the loss of potentially valuable relational information between different node types, possibly reducing the model's ability to capture complex interdependencies. The current method does not support adaptive updates, and as threat intelligence continues to evolve, timely updates and the integration of new threat data are essential for practical deployment. The authors suggest enhancing future models by extracting richer threat indicators, reducing false positives, and exploring heterogeneous graph neural networks. They also propose developing adaptive methods to ensure that the model remains effective against new and evolving threats.

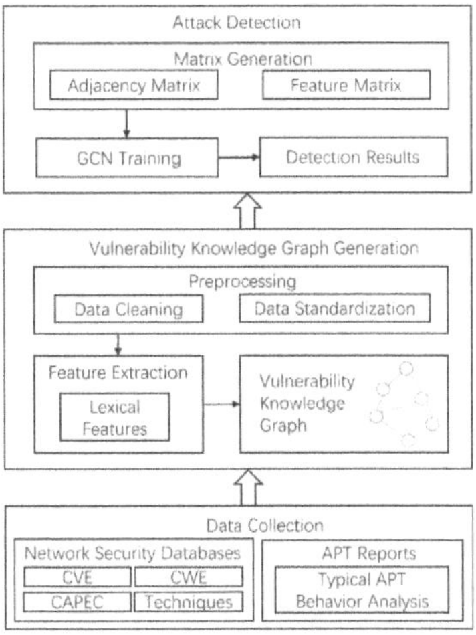

Figure 6: Architecture of the GCN-based APT Detection Model. [4]

Xiao et al. [5] propose **APT-MMF**, the first heterogeneous graph representation learning approach for *APT actor attribution* using cyber threat intelligence (CTI). Recognizing that prior attribution methods rely on a single feature type (e.g., text or tactic vectors), APT-MMF addresses the challenge of modeling rich, heterogeneous IOC (Indicator of Compromise) data found in APT reports. The system constructs a *heterogeneous attributed graph* where nodes represent reports and IOCs (e.g., malware, IPs, vulnerabilities), enriched with multimodal node features: (1) *attribute type features* (ID/ordinal encoding), (2) *natural language features* (BERT embeddings of descriptive fields), and (3) *topological relationship features* (Node2vec embeddings capturing graph structure). These features are fused via concatenation to form comprehensive node representations (see Fig. 7).

To overcome the sparse attributes of report nodes and learn deep representations for attribution, APT-MMF introduces a *triple attention mechanism.* First, *IOC type-level attention* aggregates relevant features from neighboring IOC types (e.g., malware contributes more than filenames). Then, *metapath-based neighbor node-level attention* fuses information from related reports along 20 domain-specific metapaths (e.g., shared malware or domains). Finally, *metapath semantic-level attention* assigns importance weights to each metapath to generate context-rich report embeddings. These are fed to a classifier for actor attribution. APT-MMF is trained and evaluated on a constructed heterogeneous CTI graph dataset, built from 1,300 real-world APT reports and enriched with data from STIX, ATT&CK, CVE, VirusTotal, and Avclass2. It outperforms state-of-the-art baselines (MLP, HAN, HGNN-AC) on Micro-F1 and Macro-F1 while demonstrating robustness to incomplete or noisy IOCs.

APT-MMF also emphasizes *model explainability*, showing which node types and metapaths contribute most to specific attributions, for example, domains and malware IOCs often dominate attention weights in correctly attributing Lazarus-related reports. Despite a strong performance, limitations include a reliance on complete benign IOC coverage and an inability to handle unknown actor attribution. Future work will explore the incorporation of sociopolitical indicators and open-world classification to broaden the practical deployment of this approach.

2.3.2 Provenance graph-based

2.3.2.1 Non-ML-based

Mahmoud et al. [6] present a method that converts Indicators of Compromise (IOCs) from Cyber Threat Intelligence (CTI) reports into queries for provenance graphs, enabling the detection of attacker behavior in system activity logs. Their approach bridges the gap between high-level descriptions of attack tactics, such as those found in MITRE ATT&CK or industry CTI reports, and the low-level details found in kernel audit logs collected from Linux, Windows, and FreeBSD systems. APTHunter's LogCore engine preprocesses and normalizes these raw event logs, assigning a unique identity to every system entity (such as processes and files) and capturing the relationships between them. This preprocessing step helps unify and structure the data so it can be linked back to high-level attack patterns described in CTI reports.

The core detection component, ProvQuery, translates both structured and unstructured CTI information into graph queries that can search for suspicious patterns in a Neo4j-based provenance graph. Each query is carefully constructed with elements such as the source and target entities, relevant system calls, and the sequence of process actions, reflecting how real attacks unfold. By applying these queries to the provenance graph, APTHunter treats threat hunting as a behavior-matching problem. If a query matches a pattern in the

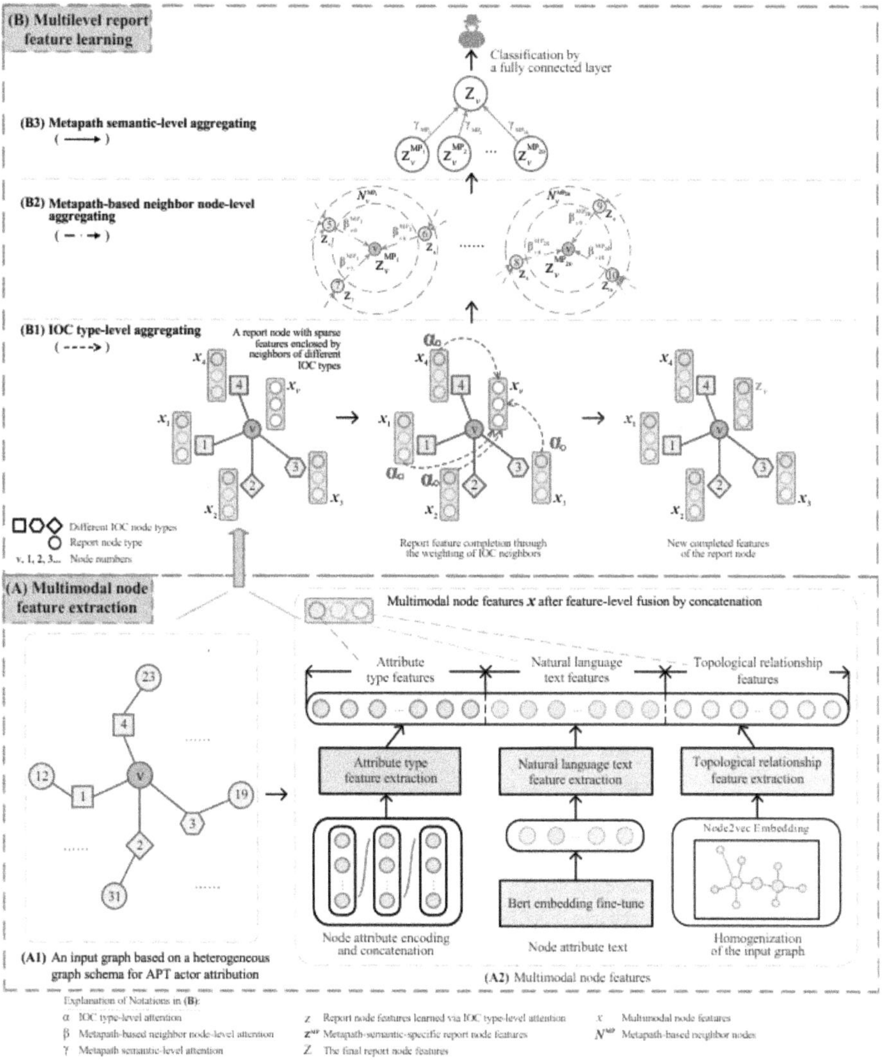

Figure 7: APT-MMF architecture: multimodal node feature extraction and multilevel attention-based feature learning over a heterogeneous attributed graph [5].

system's recent activity, the system raises an alert. Queries for different attack stages are built offline and executed in real-time as new audit data arrives, making detection both flexible and timely.
In their experiments, the authors tested APTHunter on eight multi-day APT scenarios from the DARPA Transparent Computing dataset, as well as on simulated real-world attacks based on public CTI for APT41 and APT35. For the simulated attacks, they executed real malware samples in a controlled environment and collected the resulting audit logs for analysis. The results showed that APTHunter was highly effective at detecting attacks not only in later stages, but crucially, at the earliest stages of compromise and foothold, where rapid response can stop attackers before significant damage occurs. APTHunter consistently achieved high precision and recall for these early attack stages and was able to identify malicious activity even when attackers modified surface-level artifacts while maintaining the same tactics. Additionally, during two weeks of benign enterprise activity, APTHunter generated zero false positives. The system also demonstrated strong efficiency, with a 93% reduction in memory usage compared to prior provenance-based detection approaches, making it practical for long-term, real-time deployment.
However, APTHunter's detection depends on the presence of observable malicious behaviors in the logs; attacks that rely on stolen credentials or entirely new tactics may not be detected until they leave visible traces. The system must also be updated with new queries to stay effective as attacker behaviors evolve.

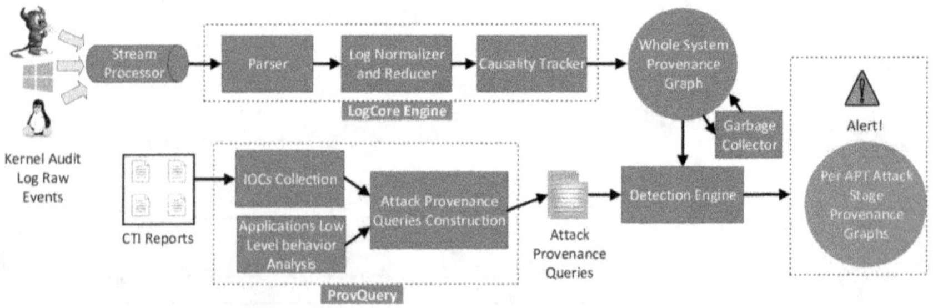

Figure 8: APTHunter system architecture [6].

Kurniawan et al. [7] propose KRYSTAL, a modular framework that unifies and enriches audit logs from Linux, FreeBSD, and Windows hosts using a standard ontology-based knowledge graph. System-call events from diverse sources are mapped into an RDF-based provenance graph using the KRYSTAL ontology, which makes system objects, their relationships, and event context explicit. This model supports semantic reasoning, easy integration of background knowledge (such as MITRE ATT&CK), and sharing across tools. To ensure scalability, the framework applies graph reduction by merging duplicate events and uses HDT-based graph compression for efficient storage and querying. The overall architecture (see Fig. 9) processes log events online and builds an enriched provenance graph for unified detection and scenario reconstruction.
KRYSTAL integrates multiple detection methods, including tag propagation, attenuation and decay (to handle dependency explosion), signature and rule-based detection from IoC definitions, and flexible graph querying by expressing all of them as SPARQL queries on the knowledge graph. This uniform knowledge graph

model enables the combination and cross-verification of various detection techniques using a standard query language, enhancing detection robustness. Provenance-based alerting policies can detect suspicious behaviors, while mapping detections to MITRE ATT&CK supports higher-level interpretation. Detected attack scenarios are reconstructed through graph pattern matching and backward-forward chaining. Experiments on five attack scenarios from the DARPA Transparent Computing datasets (Theia, Cadets, FiveDirections) demonstrate that KRYSTAL's combined methods enhance detection accuracy, facilitate efficient graph storage (resulting in up to a 66x reduction), and enable scenario reconstruction across platforms. The authors note that integrating multiple methods in a unified, ontology-driven knowledge graph not only improves detection capability and scalability but may also provide resilience against attack evasion. They highlight the potential for future enhancements such as visual query tools and distributed deployment.

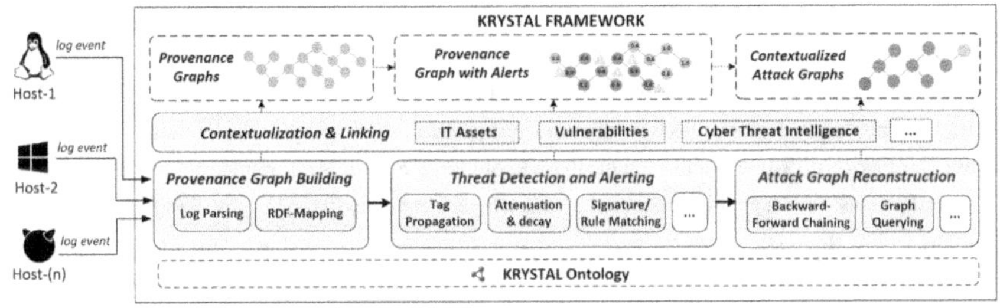

Figure 9: KRYSTAL framework architecture [7].

Wei et al. [8] present DeepHunter, a graph neural network (GNN)-based approach for robust cyber threat hunting in provenance data. DeepHunter addresses the challenge that real-world attack behaviors in provenance logs may be inconsistent with known patterns, due to system noise, missing steps, or attack mutations. To match provenance data against known behaviors, DeepHunter formulates threat hunting as a graph pattern matching task and introduces a novel architecture: an attribute embedding network uses attention to automatically learn which node attributes (such as process name, file, or IP) matter most for matching, while a graph embedding network applies two types of attention mechanisms. The first, node-level attention, determines how much information to take from each neighboring node, helping the model focus on the most relevant connections and filter out noise. The second, global context-aware attention, assigns higher weights to node embeddings that are more similar to the overall graph context, ensuring that key nodes contribute more to the final graph representation. Query graphs (representing attack behaviors from CTI) are encoded using standard GCNs, while provenance graphs are encoded with a custom network tailored for noise and redundancy; the similarity is then scored by a neural tensor network (NTN).

For evaluation, the authors use five APT attack scenarios (three real-world scenarios from the DARPA Transparent Computing dataset and two synthetic scenarios, including disconnected and mutated attack graphs), reporting three inconsistency scores: graph edit distance (GED), missing nodes, and missing paths between query and provenance graphs. DeepHunter consistently identifies all attack behaviors across scenarios and achieves stable, high matching scores (e.g., GED up to 0.557 with high accuracy), outperforming the state-of-the-art Poirot [10] and other graph matching baselines, especially in highly inconsistent or disconnected cases. It also achieves near-zero false positives and does not require expert-crafted rules, illustrating the power of attention-based GNN pattern matching for practical and robust APT threat hunting compared to non-learning graph matching approaches.

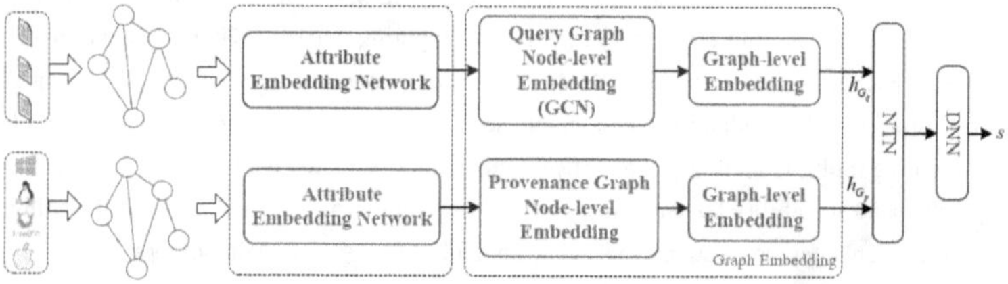

Figure 10: DeepHunter GNN-based pattern matching architecture [8].

Aly et al. [9] present MEGR-APT, a scalable and memory-efficient APT hunting system designed to process massive provenance graphs (PGs) built from system audit logs over months or years. To address the limitations of prior disk-based and memory-based solutions, MEGR-APT represents provenance data as RDF-based graphs, which enables incremental and efficient construction, querying, and long-term storage. According to Fig. 11, The system hunts APTs in two main steps: (i) it extracts suspicious subgraphs relevant to attack query graphs, which is built from CTI reports and annotated with IOC nodes, by running parallelized SPARQL queries over the RDF graph database, and (ii) it matches these subgraphs to the query graphs using a graph neural network (GNN) model for fast and robust detection. Provenance graph reduction is applied through filtering and batch processing to support scalability.

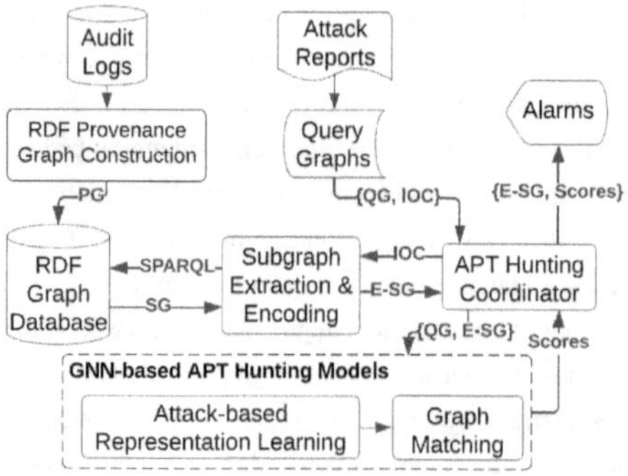

Figure 11: MEGR-APT system architecture [9].

MEGR-APT's attack-based model leverages relational graph convolutional networks (RGCN) to generate node and graph embeddings, capturing attack behaviors and the structure of surrounding nodes without manual feature engineering. Graph matching utilizes a neural tensor network (NTN) for scoring similarities between embeddings, and a global context-aware attention layer aggregates information at the graph level (see Fig. 12). For training, random benign subgraphs are generated and paired, using graph edit distance

(GED) as the supervision signal; this lets the model learn to measure similarity independently of whether a subgraph is malicious or benign. In evaluations on DARPA TC3 (TRACE, THEIA, CADETS), OpTC (Windows), and real enterprise datasets, MEGR-APT achieves up to two orders of magnitude lower memory consumption (e.g., 288MB vs. 21GB for Poirot [10], over 240GB for DeepHunter [8]) with comparable accuracy, speed, and near-zero false positives. The system is robust against variations in attack patterns and scalable for real-world, long-term APT threat hunting.

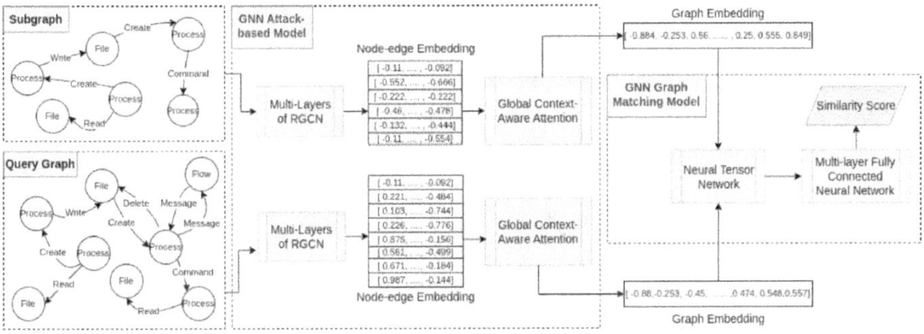

Figure 12: MEGR-APT attack-based representation learning and graph matching model [9].

Milajerdi et al. [10] present Poirot, a threat hunting system that leverages descriptive relationships from Cyber Threat Intelligence (CTI) standards to uncover the steps of complex attack campaigns. Poirot constructs a query graph from CTI data, including OpenIOC, STIX, and natural language reports, that encodes both IOCs and the relationships among them. Kernel audit logs from Linux, Windows, and FreeBSD systems are parsed to build a provenance graph representing low-level information flows and causal dependencies between system entities. Poirot then formalizes threat hunting as an inexact graph pattern matching problem, searching for subgraphs in the provenance data that align with the query graph. To enable robust and efficient detection, even with evasive or mutated attacks, Poirot introduces a novel influence score metric to prioritize the most attacker-relevant flows, mitigating the dependency explosion problem. Figure 13 illustrates the system architecture.

The core alignment algorithm in Poirot begins by finding candidate node alignments between the query and provenance graphs, expanding from the seed node with the highest likelihood of a true match. The search explores paths in the provenance graph that may correspond to single edges in the query, allowing for noise and partial matches. Each candidate alignment receives a similarity score based on the structural and contextual fit between the graphs; if the score exceeds a threshold, Poirot raises an alert and provides a report for forensic analysis. Poirot was evaluated on ten attack scenarios from the DARPA Transparent Computing dataset and real-world incident reports across Linux, Windows, and FreeBSD operating systems. Results show Poirot reliably detects all attacks, maintains high accuracy with low false positives on multi-million-node graphs, and often completes searches in minutes, outperforming traditional IOC scanners by leveraging the structure of CTI relationships and graph dependencies.

Hossain et al. [11] propose MORSE, a provenance-based APT detection framework designed to combat

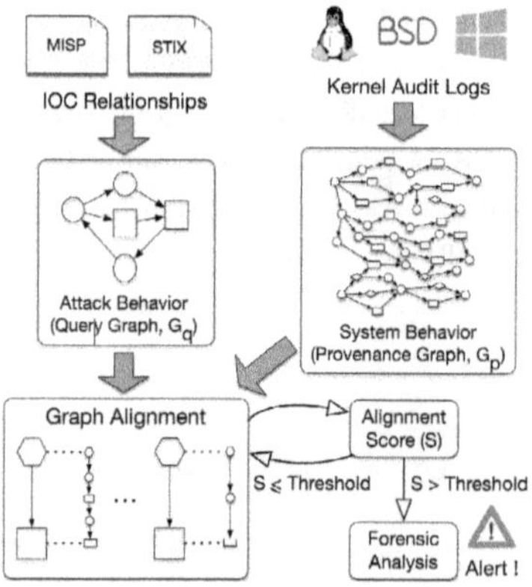

Figure 13: Poirot system architecture [10].

the dependence explosion problem in forensic analysis. Traditional IOC-based and provenance approaches often trigger a flood of false positives in enterprise-scale systems, as attacks are rare events that are often hidden among billions of benign actions. Moreover, existing tools usually only connect individual suspicious events, making it difficult for analysts to see the high-level campaign and "connect the dots" across multi-step attacks. MORSE addresses these challenges by introducing tag-based prioritization and propagation rules that focus the analysis on a manageable subset of dependencies relevant to likely attack paths.

MORSE assigns real-valued data tags (integrity and confidentiality) and subject tags (benign, trusted, suspicious code, suspicious environment) to nodes in the provenance graph. Its core innovation is to modulate tag propagation with two mechanisms: *tag attenuation* (reducing suspicion when benign subjects propagate data) and *tag decay* (gradually lifting suspicion if no malicious behavior is observed). These rules are conservative for suspicious processes, propagating low-integrity tags aggressively, but lenient for benign ones, greatly reducing the spread of alarms and the size of resulting scenario graphs. Detection policies are defined over a small set of provenance-derived conditions and are enforced using a domain-specific event language. In experiments on DARPA Transparent Computing datasets (Ubuntu, FreeBSD; TC3 engagement), MORSE achieved an $11.4\times$ reduction in alarms and a $35\times$ reduction in scenario graph size on average compared to previous provenance systems, while maintaining high detection coverage. The framework successfully reconstructed compact scenario graphs for stealthy APTs, including in-memory and kernel-resident malware, lateral movement, and rootkits and operated efficiently with low memory usage (about 1 byte per event) and millisecond-level detection times. These results demonstrate that conservative tag propagation and targeted scenario reconstruction deliver robust, scalable, and analyst-friendly APT detection in real-world environments.

HOLMES [12] presents a real-time system for Advanced Persistent Threat (APT) detection that correlates suspicious information flows across multiple hosts using audit logs from Linux, FreeBSD, and Windows. The main technical challenge tackled by HOLMES is bridging the semantic gap between low-level audit logs and the high-level kill-chain abstraction of attacker behavior. To achieve this, HOLMES represents audit events

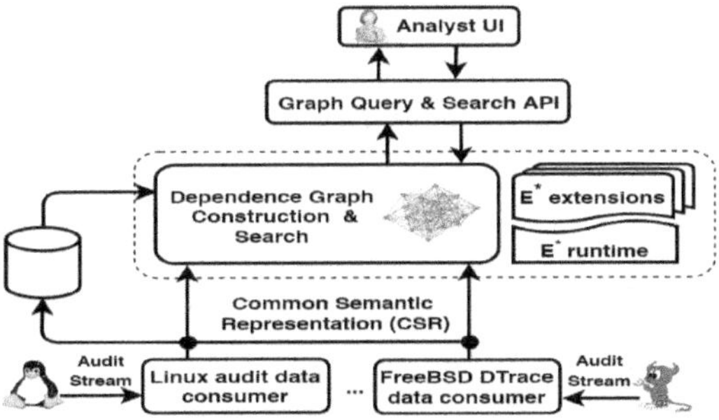

Figure 14: MORSE system architecture [11].

as a provenance graph in main memory, then uses an intermediate layer based on the MITRE ATT&CK framework to match Tactics, Techniques, and Procedures (TTPs) as subgraphs within the provenance graph. This process enables mapping low-level system activities to high-level attack stages, efficiently matching low-level events to TTPs, and detecting correlations among attack steps.

A core innovation in HOLMES is the construction of the High-level Scenario Graph (HSG), which provides a compact, real-time summary of an ongoing attack campaign. Each node in the HSG corresponds to a matched TTP, and edges represent causality or information flow dependencies among TTPs. The system incorporates several design features to reduce false positives, including noise filtering through learned benign prerequisites, benign data flow quantity thresholds, and a severity-based ranking mechanism for HSGs. HOLMES employs an incremental matching algorithm for TTPs, allowing efficient processing without expensive backtracking. This architecture, illustrated in Figure 15, supports platform-independent, OS-neutral log processing and can scale to large enterprise environments.

HOLMES was evaluated using nine real-world APT scenarios across Ubuntu, FreeBSD, and Windows systems, leveraging kernel audit data from the DARPA Transparent Computing program. The attacks covered classic APT activities, including drive-by compromise, privilege escalation, lateral movement, and exfiltration. The evaluation showed that HOLMES separates benign and attack scenarios with high precision and recall (accuracy = recall = 1 in tested datasets), and with a low false positive rate. Notably, HOLMES reduced the volume of analyzed events by mapping millions of audit records to compact, high-level graphs and demonstrated the ability to support hundreds of hosts in real-time. The results highlight that HOLMES effectively correlates suspicious information flows and provides actionable, high-level summaries of attacks for analysts.

Liu et al. [13] propose Log2vec, a modular approach for detecting insider threats and APTs in enterprise environments by transforming system logs into a heterogeneous graph. Unlike most prior methods focused only on sequential relationships among log entries, Log2vec encodes richer relationships, including causal and sequential links within a day, logical connections across days, and object-based relationships among hosts and files by applying heuristic rules to parsed meta-attributes (subject, object, operation type, time, host) from each entry. The system's architecture (see Fig. 16) consists of three modules: log-to-graph con-

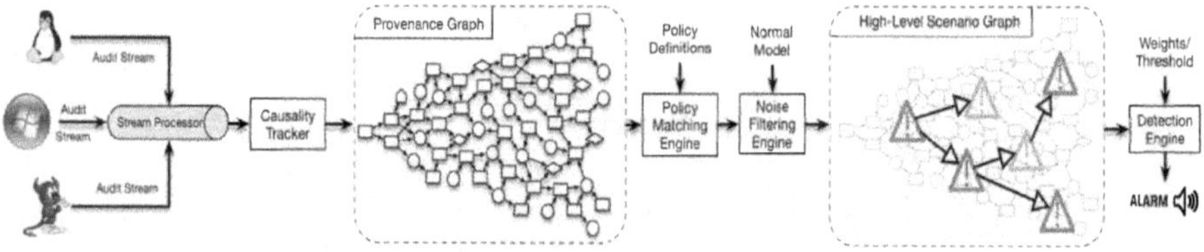

Figure 15: HOLMES architecture: From audit logs to high-level attack scenario graph (adapted from [12]).

version, graph embedding, and clustering-based anomaly detection.

In the embedding phase, Log2vec applies random walks on the heterogeneous graph, followed by a skip-gram (word2vec) model to obtain low-dimensional vector representations of log entries, capturing both immediate and long-range context. The resulting vectors are clustered; small clusters typically indicate rare or anomalous activity, and these are flagged as suspicious. This unsupervised approach requires no labeled attack data, making it robust and adaptable to varied user behaviors and attack types.

Log2vec was evaluated on the CERT Insider Threat dataset (five scenarios, six malicious users) and the LANL dataset (98 attackers). Experimental results demonstrate that Log2vec outperforms state-of-the-art methods, including DeepLog, TIRESIAS, and HMM, in terms of AUC and precision, particularly for detecting rare and fine-grained attack events. Its flexible modeling of log relationships enables high accuracy, though some false positives remain due to behavioral diversity.

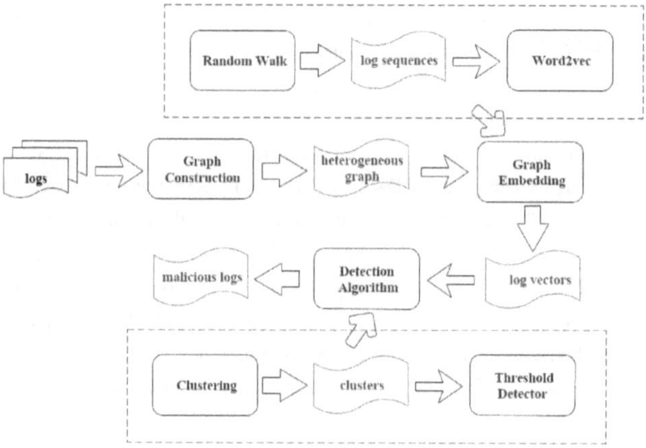

Figure 16: Log2vec system architecture: from log parsing and heterogeneous graph construction to graph embedding and clustering-based detection [13].

Li et al. [14] propose ProvGRP, a context-aware provenance graph reduction and partition approach that addresses the significant challenge of redundant and voluminous audit logs in attack investigation. While previous audit log reduction methods rely on rigid, template-based filtering and often ignore rich contextual event information, they struggle to eliminate false dependencies caused by the coarse granularity of logs. This makes attack investigations difficult, expensive, and prone to both missed evidence and analyst overload. ProvGRP is designed to overcome these limitations by reducing graph size while preserving behavior-relevant information, thus serving as a practical and accurate preprocessing step for downstream attack analysis.

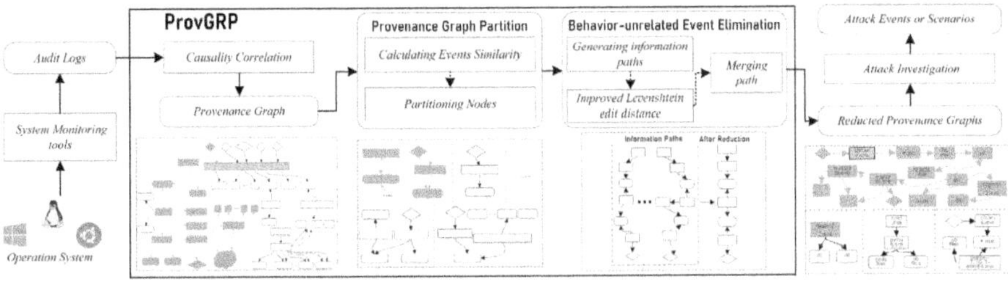

Figure 17: Overview of the ProvGRP workflow: construction, partitioning, and reduction of provenance graphs [14].

The ProvGRP workflow (see Figure 17) consists of three key components: (1) provenance graph construction from platform-independent audit logs using causality correlation, (2) graph partitioning to separate long-running process nodes using event features, and (3) behavior-unrelated event elimination by merging similar information paths. ProvGRP uses three core features to partition events: the time interval between events (events within the same behavior tend to have smaller time intervals), entity name similarity (subjects or objects in the same behavior are typically similar), and operation type similarity (only a limited set of operations is observed per behavior). Based on the insight that information paths from the same high-level behavior share similar flow patterns, ProvGRP generates context-rich information paths and iteratively merges paths with similar flow patterns using an improved Levenshtein distance metric (see Figure 18). This process eliminates false dependencies and merges redundant events, resulting in a reduced and more interpretable provenance graph.

Evaluation on two public datasets, namely ATLAS and DARPA CADETS, shows that ProvGRP achieves substantial reduction factors (10.10× for ATLAS and 42.21× for CADETS), high partition accuracy (0.805 to 0.954), and preserves crucial attack information (attack information loss below 0.1). ProvGRP not only outperforms state-of-the-art reduction methods in accuracy and data reduction, but also decreases the runtime of subsequent attack investigations (reducing runtime by 34.4% on ATLAS and 61.0% on CADETS), with only a marginal decrease in recall and F1-score.

Wang et al. [15] present THREATRACE, a real-time, semi-supervised anomaly detection framework for node-level host-based threat detection within provenance graphs. Unlike methods that require prior knowledge of attack patterns, THREATRACE is trained only on benign data and thus does not employ a traditional binary classification approach. The system operates in a streaming mode, continually appending incoming nodes and edges from audit logs (e.g., CamFlow) to a disk-based provenance graph, while maintaining a subgraph of active and related nodes in memory to ensure scalability for long-term monitoring.

THREATRACE tailors GraphSAGE, an inductive graph neural network (GNN), to learn the behavioral roles

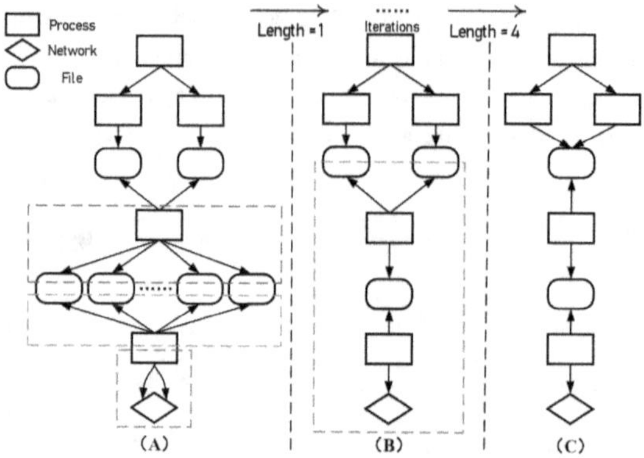

Figure 18: Example of information path merging in ProvGRP [14].

of benign nodes by extracting features as the distribution of different edge types for each node. The intuition is that a node's behavior is reflected in the structure and types of its immediate relationships. Nodes are labeled by type (e.g., process, file, socket), and during training, the entire graph is divided into manageable subgraphs (e.g., 150,000 active nodes and their neighborhoods per subgraph), allowing only one subgraph to be in memory at a time. To address severe class imbalance and capture hidden roles within node types, THREATRACE introduces a multi-model framework. After training a submodel, correctly classified nodes are removed, and the remaining nodes are used for subsequent submodel training. A node is considered benign if at least one submodel classifies it as such; otherwise, it is labeled as anomalous. This iterative approach allows the model to capture both dominant and rare behaviors within each node type.

To reduce false positives, THREATRACE uses both a waiting time threshold and a tolerant threshold before raising alerts, allowing temporary anomalies to resolve naturally. The final system provides precise tracing of anomalous nodes, enabling analysts to directly investigate the source and context of suspicious activity (see Figure 19). Evaluation on five public datasets, including StreamSpot, Unicorn SC-1/SC-2, and DARPA TC, demonstrates that THREATRACE outperforms state-of-the-art detectors (such as Unicorn, ProvDetector, and Log2vec) in both precision and recall, especially when threat-related entities are rare. The framework is effective in early-phase attack detection, robust to evasion, and scales to enterprise-level, long-term deployment.

Zhu et al. [16] propose APTSHIELD, a stable and real-time APT detection system for Linux hosts that addresses the challenges of weak data source integrity, high processing overhead, and poor scalability in existing solutions. The architecture (see Fig. 20) comprises three modules: auditd-based data collection, data compaction, and an ATT&CK-inspired APT detection framework. A core contribution of APTSHIELD is its real-time data compaction strategy, which is achieved through redundant semantics skipping (removing repeated events by tracking the latest process semantics) and non-viable entity pruning (removing inactive or irrelevant nodes). This dramatically reduces memory and computational overhead, ensuring stable operation over long periods.

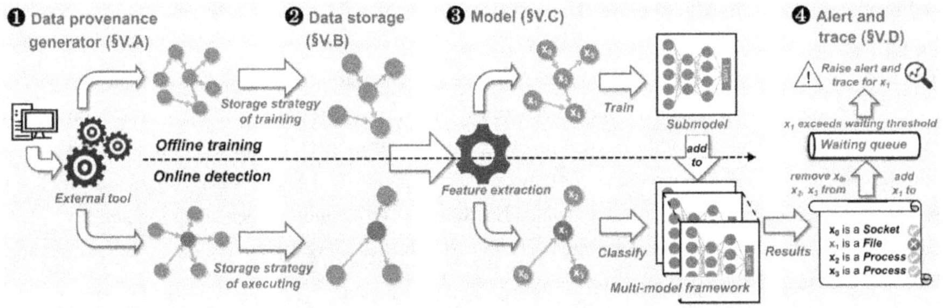

Figure 19: Overview of THREATRACE architecture and multi-model detection process [15].

The detection framework assigns status and behavior labels to processes, and untrusted/high-value labels to files. These labels are transferred and aggregated through control and data flow relationships, following the MITRE ATT&CK model. Control flow labels propagate through process creation and inheritance. In contrast, data flow labels track the paths of untrusted or high-value information, enabling the accurate association of multi-stage attacks and the reconstruction of the attack chain for forensic analysis.

Evaluations on both laboratory and DARPA Engagement datasets show that APTSHIELD detects diverse attack types (webshell, fileless attacks, and remote access trojans) with low false favorable rates and efficiency superior to related systems, such as Conan, Sleuth, and HOLMES. It achieves approximately 20–35% reduction in data volume, maintains constant memory usage even on long-running systems, and processes events in real time (up to 309 times faster than event generation). These results highlight APTSHIELD's effectiveness in protecting real-world Linux hosts.

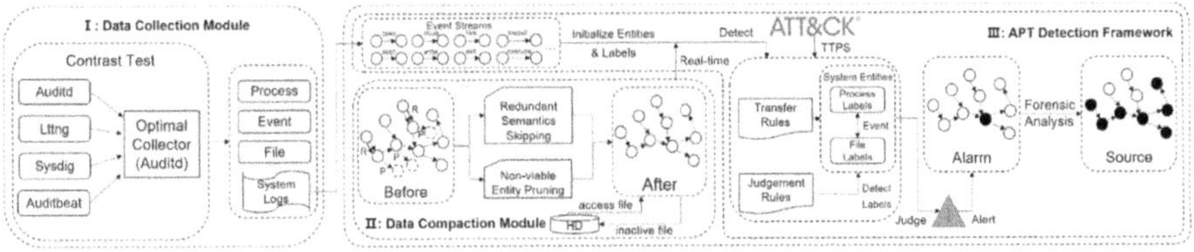

Figure 20: APTSHIELD architecture: Data collection, compaction, and ATT&CK-based detection [16].

2.3.2.2 ML-based

Afnan et al. [17] propose *LogShield*, a transformer-based framework to detect APT attacks from provenance-based event traces. The authors address key limitations in prior approaches: traditional deep learning techniques for APT detection (such as LSTMs) experience severe performance degradation as the volume and length of event sequences increase, while transformer-based models, though more scalable, are ineffective when fed raw log data because they often miss critical indicators of malicious activity. To overcome these issues, LogShield introduces a generalized preprocessing pipeline that extracts and encodes crucial context and temporal relationships from provenance graphs, ensuring that important attack semantics are preserved for the model.

The system architecture (see Fig. 21) involves generating event traces by traversing provenance graphs, encoding each event as object-action and time-difference tokens, and passing these through custom embedding layers before classification with a RoBERTa-based transformer model. The model is trained using cross-entropy loss, employs a sliding window for temporal segmentation, and balances class distribution by down-sampling benign traces. This approach enables LogShield's self-attention mechanism to learn both global and local dependencies in attack patterns, capturing APT tactics more effectively than previous methods, albeit with increased memory and computation overhead.

Results on the DARPA OpTC and TC E3 datasets show LogShield outperforms LSTM and previous language models for long and complex traces, though a few shorter traces are still better detected by LSTM, suggesting that transformers can sometimes overlook highly local sequential patterns that LSTM models can exploit. The authors identify several future directions for LogShield: (1) pretraining the model on larger datasets. Since only three hosts from the DARPA OpTC dataset were used, expanding to more hosts may further improve performance; (2) upgrading the preprocessing architecture to capture crucial features better; and (3) improving prediction performance through more thorough hyperparameter tuning, such as using grid search to optimize model parameters.

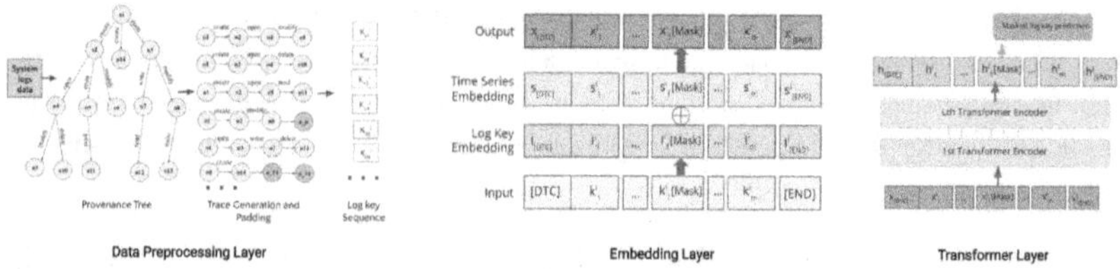

Figure 21: LogShield pipeline: provenance-based event trace extraction, temporal embedding, and transformer-based detection [17].

Alsaheel et al. [18] introduce ATLAS, a framework for reconstructing end-to-end attack stories from system audit logs by learning generalized attack strategies. The key insight is that diverse attacks often share similar abstract patterns at the entity-action level, across processes, files, and network connections, regardless of exploited vulnerabilities or payloads. To address the limitations of existing graph-based forensic tools, which generate massive and complex dependency graphs that remain hard to interpret and depend on expert-defined rules, ATLAS leverages causality analysis, NLP, and LSTM-based sequence modeling. Audit logs are converted into optimized causal graphs, and lemmatized, temporally ordered event sequences are extracted. Levenshtein Distance-based undersampling and mutation-based oversampling balance the attack and non-attack data. Word embeddings encode the sequence context for the LSTM, enabling the model to distinguish between attacks and benign behavior more robustly than anomaly-based methods, which often suffer from high false positives as user behaviors evolve.

During inference, an analyst supplies an attack symptom entity (alert), from which ATLAS extracts candidate event sequences from the causal graph. The LSTM-based sequence model predicts which entities participate in the attack and recovers the relevant, temporally ordered steps as an attack story (Fig. 22). ATLAS supports both single- and multi-host attacks, demonstrating strong improvements over traditional rule-based or graph-traversal approaches. This substantially reduces analyst workload and data volume while uncovering generalized attack strategies that cut across specific exploits or payloads.

However, ATLAS has notable limitations. It requires analysts to provide a true attack-symptom entity for each investigation, which is a significant practical barrier, as such ground truth is rarely available in real incidents. If a false positive is used as input, only benign or irrelevant events will be returned. ATLAS also requires an initial list of manually designated attack entities for training, which is a one-time but non-trivial labeling effort. The authors acknowledge these constraints and plan future work to extend ATLAS to support diverse audit log formats and enhance its sequence labeling and model tuning for broader applicability.

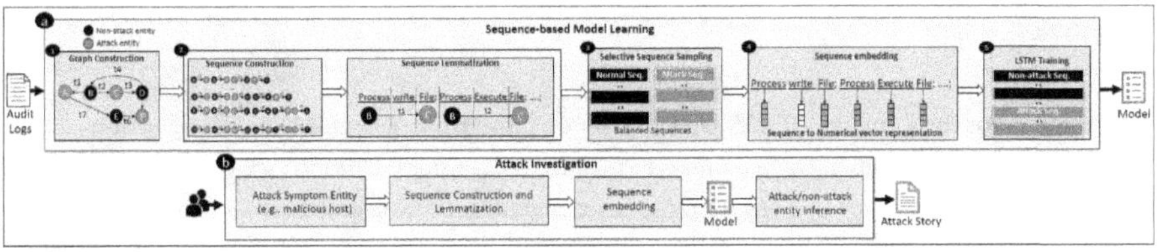

Figure 22: Overview of the ATLAS architecture [18].

Sun et al. [19] propose DEEPRO. This provenance-based detection framework precisely identifies attack-relevant entities. It reconstructs APT campaigns in provenance graphs, overcoming limitations of prior methods that require expert-defined rules or cannot pinpoint attack events. DEEPRO's workflow comprises three main steps: (1) provenance graph construction and preprocessing, (2) a customized heterogeneous GNN model for process node detection, and (3) campaign entity correlation and recovery (see Fig. 23). In preprocessing, the system applies graph compression to remove redundant, read-only, or isolated nodes and merges duplicate edges, focusing analysis on attack-relevant activity.

Node features for processes, files, and networks are initialized with Doc2vec and mapped to a unified space using type-specific linear transformation. DEEPRO employs a metapath-aggregation-based GNN (MAGNN) to capture heterogeneous node relationships and semantic/structural correlations, with three metapaths explicitly designed to model causality among processes. Attention mechanisms (see Fig. 24) learn the importance of different metapaths, addressing the intuition that certain attack behaviors (such as frequent process forking or file access) are more suspicious than others. Within the MAGNN, LeakyReLU is used as the activation function to handle negative values better and provide non-linearity for node representation learning. At the same time, softmax is applied to normalize the attention weights across multiple metapaths, ensuring their relative importance is effectively modeled. Training utilizes both weighted cross-entropy loss (for addressing class imbalance) and supervised contrastive loss (for enhancing the separation of attack and benign processes in the learned space). After detecting attack-relevant process nodes, DEEPRO correlates them through control and data dependencies to reconstruct the APT campaign, and then identifies attack-relevant files and networks based on their interactions with multiple malicious processes.

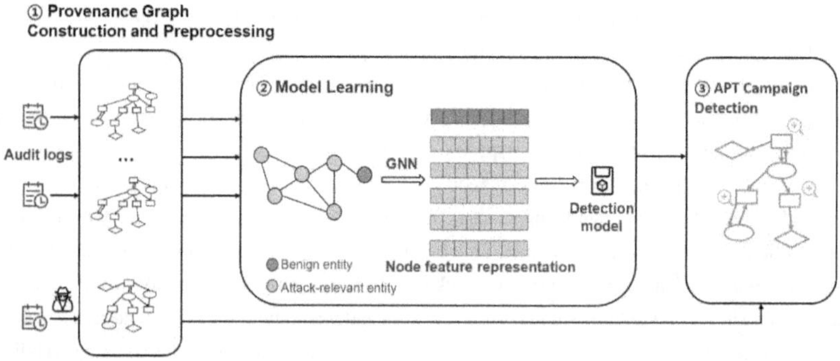

Figure 23: Overview of the DEEPRO framework: preprocessing, GNN-based process node detection, and APT campaign recovery [19].

Evaluation is conducted on the ATLAS public Windows provenance dataset [51], requiring high-quality labeled attack entities for training (a one-time but essential manual step). DEEPRO shows improved detection and campaign reconstruction compared to rule-based and prior GNN approaches. Limitations include dependence on labeled training data and the lack of validation on other platforms. Future work will expand to more datasets and explore self-supervised or unsupervised learning for scalability.

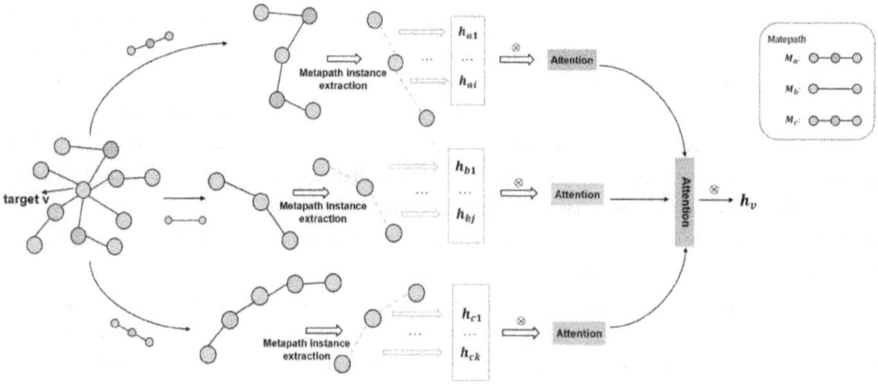

Figure 24: DEEPRO's metapath aggregation and attention mechanism: modeling and weighting process-file-process and process-network-process relationships for campaign detection [19].

Yang et al. [20] propose AISL, an attack intent-driven and sequence-based learning framework to address the scarcity of positive APT samples and the integration of heterogeneous audit data for APT detection. AISL creates a provenance graph in RDF format, utilizing direct mapping and R2RM, from multiple sources, including system and network audit logs. During graph construction, each node is assigned both a trustworthiness (integrity) tag and a confidentiality tag, with values such as Benign And Authentic (BA), Benign

(BE), Unknown (UN), Secret (SC), Private (PR), and Public (PU), leveraging existing whitelists and private data (which is itself a limitation if such curated data is not available in practice). The AISL architecture consists of two main modules: (1) tag-sequence-based semantic model training and (2) attack detection (see Fig. 25). First, the provenance graph is preprocessed to prune unreachable entities, consolidate redundant edges, and merge duplicate or granular events. Attack and non-attack event sequences are constructed by collecting the chronological actions of attack and non-attack entities, converting them to lemmatized text. To address class imbalance, AISL employs similarity-based undersampling for non-attack sequences and mutation-based oversampling for attack sequences, thereby ensuring a balanced training dataset.

For semantic model training, sequences are input to a deep learning architecture composed of a dropout layer for regularization, a 1D convolutional (Conv1D) layer with max pooling for extracting sequence features, and fully connected dense layers with sigmoid activations for output. AISL incorporates an LSTM layer after the Conv1D layer, enabling the model to capture both short-term and long-term dependencies in the sequence data, which is crucial for learning complex attack patterns that span over time. During detection, when the system receives an alert (e.g., from a blocklisted IP or suspicious entity), it constructs candidate entity sets and corresponding sequences, passing them through the LSTM-based model to classify them as attack or benign.

Experimental evaluation demonstrates that AISL outperforms baseline methods in terms of detection rate and favorable sample coverage, particularly in scenarios with limited labeled attacks, and is robust across multiple heterogeneous audit data sources. However, practical limitations include reliance on curated whitelist/private data for tagging, dependence on external alert sources to trigger detection, and the need for manual labeling of attack intent.

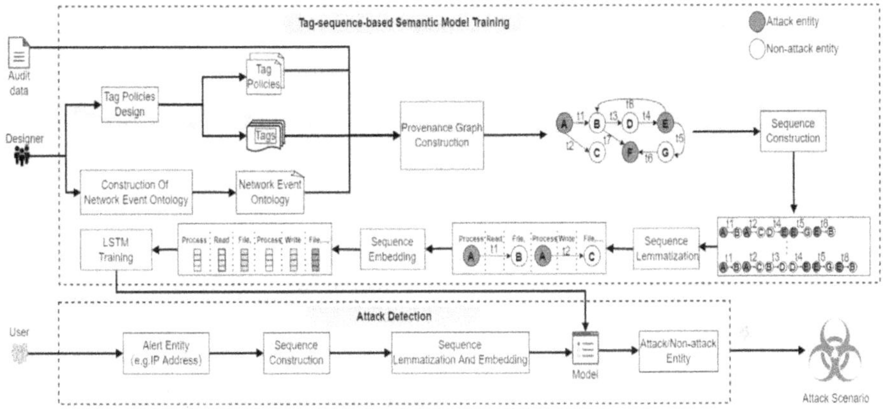

Figure 25: AISL architecture: heterogeneous audit integration, provenance graph tagging, tag-sequence generation, and LSTM-based semantic model training and detection [20].

Zhang et al. [21] present KAIROS, the first provenance-based intrusion detection system (PIDS) to simultaneously satisfy four key desiderata: detection scope (cross-application and boundary-spanning attacks), attack agnosticity (detection of novel attacks without prior knowledge), timeliness (efficient streaming detection), and attack reconstruction (automatic summarization for forensic analysis). Existing PIDS approaches typically compromise one or more of these objectives, while KAIROS achieves all four by combining deep graph learning and community discovery in a streaming setting.

KAIROS employs a novel GNN-based encoder-decoder architecture that analyzes the temporal evolution of provenance graphs (see Fig. 26). For each new edge ingested from the audit stream, an encoder (using a Temporal Graph Network, TGN) computes edge embeddings based on the local neighborhood structure and node states, where each node state is a hierarchical feature hash encoding its historical context and semantic similarity (e.g., files in the same directory are mapped close together). The decoder, implemented as a multilayer perceptron (MLP), reconstructs the edge type from the embedding. Reconstruction error is used to quantify event anomalousness. KAIROS processes the provenance graph in time windows, maintaining queues of overlapping windows; a queue is flagged as anomalous if its cumulative reconstruction error exceeds a threshold. This provides fine-grained, periodic anomaly detection without prior knowledge of attack signatures.

Attack reconstruction is accomplished by clustering high-error edges into dense communities using the Louvain algorithm, automatically generating compact summary graphs (Using GraphViz) that distill malicious activity for analyst review. A node is marked as suspicious if it is incident to an edge with high reconstruction error (anomalousness) and is rare (seldom observed in benign runs). KAIROS's approach is robust even when attacks are buried within extensive benign data and is agnostic to specific attack characteristics. Experiments on DARPA datasets demonstrate that KAIROS can accurately detect hidden attacks and distill large provenance graphs into concise, meaningful attack summaries, significantly aiding forensic triage. In contrast, benign graphs typically exhibit small, well-bounded process communities. By bridging deep temporal graph learning and community detection, KAIROS advances the practicality of streaming, real-time, attack-agnostic provenance-based intrusion detection.

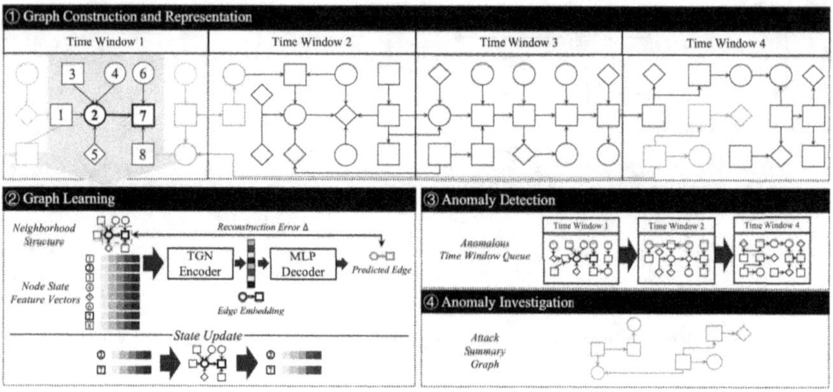

Figure 26: Overview of the KAIROS architecture: streaming edge ingestion, GNN-based encoder-decoder, anomaly detection, and summary graph generation [21].

Sun et al. [22] propose ProcSAGE, an efficient and accurate host-based APT detection framework leveraging graph representation learning on provenance data. Unlike prior provenance-based approaches that monitor all entities (processes, files, sockets), ProcSAGE narrows the focus to process and thread nodes, significantly reducing graph scale and computational overhead. This is motivated by the observation that attacks typically manifest as abnormal process behaviors, and that process nodes are significantly fewer in number than files/sockets, making targeted monitoring more tractable and efficient.

The ProcSAGE pipeline comprises (1) provenance graph construction from host audit logs, (2) subgraph extraction based on syscall types (to address graph heterogeneity), and (3) process feature extraction. Semantic features (process name, syscall frequencies in a time window) and topological features (average neighbor degree and local clustering coefficient within two hops) are computed and concatenated for each process node. These are input to a GraphSAGE model with mean aggregation and ReLU activation, trained to generate embeddings that cluster same-labeled processes closely in Euclidean space (using a cross-entropy loss and a K-means-inspired iterative optimization). Outlier detection is then performed via both fixed and relative distance thresholds in embedding space, flagging anomalous processes. The overall ProcSAGE architecture is shown in Fig. 27.

ProcSAGE achieves high accuracy and low cost, requiring no expert knowledge or handcrafted rules, and is robust to massive audit logs due to its resource-efficient design. Experiments demonstrate its superior performance and scalability compared to existing provenance-based methods. However, focusing solely on processes may potentially miss attacks that exploit file/socket-only behaviors, and the technique relies on audit log granularity and correct windowing for syscall frequency features.

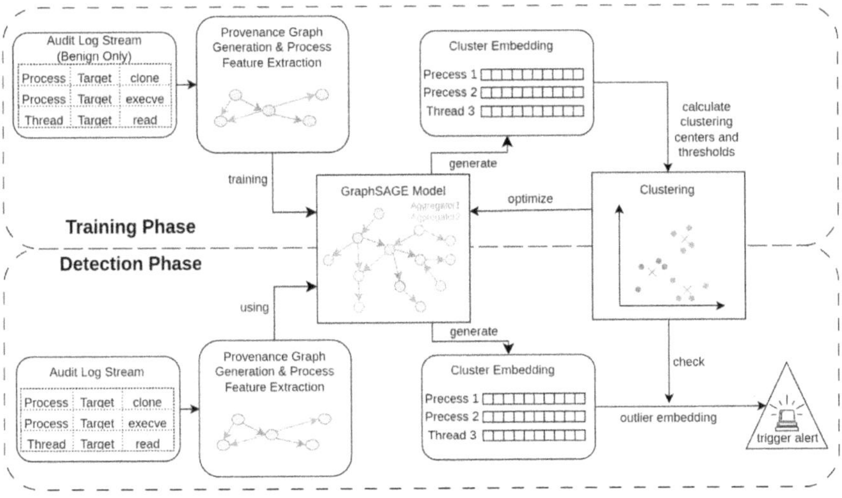

Figure 27: Overview of ProcSAGE architecture: process-centric provenance graph construction, feature extraction, GraphSAGE-based clustering, and anomaly detection [22].

Das et al. [23] propose Prov2vec, a provenance-based system for continuous and early detection of Advanced

Persistent Threats (APTs) by monitoring enterprise host behavior. The key innovation is a provenance graph kernel that captures the canonical structure of system activity over time, producing compact and discriminative representations for unsupervised detection tasks. As shown in Fig. 28, Prov2vec operates by periodically taking snapshots of the system's provenance graph, then constructing node label histograms using label-aware backward walks (with tunable neighborhood size to capture local/global behaviors). To reduce graph size and avoid dependency explosion, causality-preserving duplicate elimination and node versioning are applied during snapshot creation. The node label histograms are efficiently encoded into fixed-size feature vectors using a probabilistic data structure, histosketch, which supports streaming and incremental comparison as the vocabulary of node labels grows.

These compact graph representations are then fed to a suite of unsupervised machine learning models. The evaluation includes: (1) *graph classification*, where the system distinguishes benign from malicious activity using support vector machines (SVM) and random forests; (2) *outlier detection*, using Local Outlier Factor and One-Class SVM to spot unusual host behavior; and (3) *graph clustering*, grouping host behaviors to uncover latent attack patterns. Across all tasks, Prov2vec's kernel achieves higher detection accuracy and efficiency than previous embedding methods, enabling early APT detection in large-scale, streaming enterprise settings. There are, however, notable limitations: Prov2vec operates under a *closed-world assumption*, presuming all benign behaviors are observed during training, which is an unrealistic condition in real enterprise networks, which may lead to false alarms for previously unseen normal activities. Furthermore, as with most black-box machine learning approaches, *explainability of anomalies is limited*, and Prov2vec may struggle to provide detailed explanations for why an anomaly was detected.

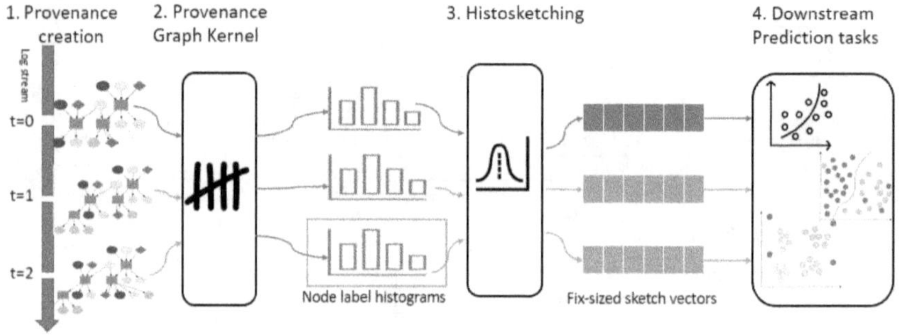

Figure 28: Prov2vec architecture: provenance graph snapshotting, histogram construction, histosketch feature extraction, and unsupervised detection [23].

Zhang et al. [24] address the challenges of prior provenance-based APT detection, including the need for a priori knowledge, lack of attack data, and high computational overhead, by proposing APT-MGL, a self-supervised learning-based model for detecting malicious nodes in provenance graphs. As shown in Fig. 29, APT-MGL's architecture includes: (1) log preprocessing, (2) node feature extraction and embedding, (3) multi-head self-attention feature fusion with masked graph representation learning, and (4) node clustering and outlier detection.

APT-MGL considers three types of node features: node types, node behavioral features (captured from sequences of interactions, encoded using word2vec with temporal encoding), and node degree features (in/out-degree to different edge types). After embedding these features, a multi-head self-attention mechanism fuses them, providing high-quality representations that capture different semantic information in the data, for the graph neural network. The core is GraphMAE2, a masked graph self-encoder that learns node embeddings by masking and reconstructing parts of the graph during training, thereby capturing intricate relationships and dependencies in a self-supervised manner. The decoder, based on GAT (Graph Attention Networks), reconstructs the original graph structures and features, utilizing stochastic masking in decoding to enhance model robustness and mitigate overfitting. Node anomaly detection is finally performed using KNN clustering on the learned embeddings.

APT-MGL requires only benign audit logs for training and adapts over time by incorporating new normal data via self-supervised adaptation. Experimental results show that APT-MGL outperforms existing provenance-based and monitoring approaches in terms of accuracy and efficiency, with a low computational cost. However, the model assumes all benign system behaviors are captured in the training data (closed-world assumption), which may limit its ability to handle unseen benign activity and lead to false alarms. In addition, APT-MGL focuses on node-level detection and localization of attacks but does not interpret or classify attack types, suggesting directions for future work to enhance attack recovery and context-aware interpretation.

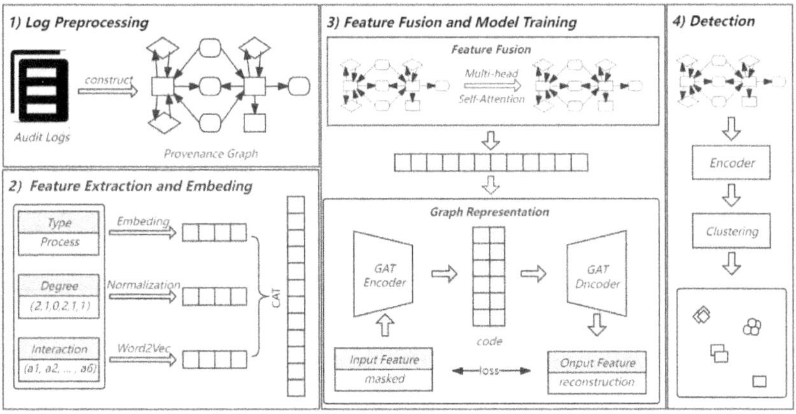

Figure 29: APT-MGL architecture: log preprocessing, node feature embedding and fusion, masked graph self-encoder (GraphMAE2), and anomaly detection [24].

Jiang et al. [25] propose RT-APT, a real-time anomaly detection framework for Advanced Persistent Threats (APTs) operating on large-scale provenance graphs. RT-APT is designed to overcome key challenges faced by prior APT detection methods, such as high computational overhead, limited generality, and heavy reliance on expert rules. The architecture (see Fig. 30) comprises three modules: (1) data acquisition and preprocessing via the SPADE tool to collect Linux kernel audit logs, (2) graph feature extraction, and (3) real-time anomaly detection. For feature extraction, RT-APT first builds provenance graphs from kernel logs and embeds node context using the Weisfeiler-Lehman (WL) subtree kernel. The WL subtree kernel iteratively aggregates neighborhood information to form efficient node histograms that reflect the causal structures of system execution. This method is chosen over alternatives like the random walk kernel, which may overlook important deterministic causal structures, and the shortest-path kernel, which can miss subtle contextual differences, because WL provides an optimal trade-off between speed and expressiveness for provenance-based system modeling.

After embedding, RT-APT applies the FlexSketch algorithm to handle the streaming nature of provenance graphs. FlexSketch transforms the high-dimensional histograms into fixed-size graph sketches, supporting fast and incremental updates. Critically, FlexSketch enables RT-APT to address concept drift, i.e., the evolving nature of expected system behavior over time. By dynamically updating the sketch representations and "forgetting" outdated data when necessary, RT-APT ensures robust and adaptive detection, even as benign activity patterns shift. During training, the system uses K-means clustering on sequences of benign graph sketches, where each cluster represents a different normal system state, such as the startup state, initialization state, and stable state.

At runtime, each new feature vector is compared to all clusters and sub-models. If a sketch fits an existing cluster, it is marked benign; otherwise, it is flagged as an anomaly. RT-APT also tracks transitions between clusters, if an observed transition has not previously occurred during training (i.e., an "invalid transition"), this is considered anomalous as well. This dual detection mechanism allows RT-APT to recognize both unknown behaviors and unusual context shifts. Experimental results on StreamSpot, Unicorn, and laboratory datasets demonstrate that RT-APT outperforms state-of-the-art techniques in terms of runtime, memory, and CPU efficiency. Nevertheless, the system assumes an initial phase of secure model training (potentially resulting in false positives with novel benign behaviors). It may require careful parameter tuning, especially when handling very complex data streams.

Table 1: Summary of APT Detection Studies

Authors	Proposed Name	Objective	OS	Preprocessing	Model	Dataset	Results
Mahmoud et al. (2023)	APTHunter	Early-stage APT detection via CTI-based provenance queries	Linux Windows FreeBSD	Build provenance graph, entity unification	Attack provenance queries	DARPA TC3, APT41/ APT35 simulation	High early-stage precision/recall; zero false positives; 93% less memory
Kurniawan et al. (2022)	KRYSTAL	Modular APT detection and scenario reconstruction via RDF knowledge graph	Linux FreeBSD Windows	Log parsing, RDF mapping, deduplication, HDT compression	Tag propagation, attenuation and decay, SPARQL rules/signature, graph querying	DARPA TC (5 scenarios)	Combined detection improves accuracy; up to 66x graph reduction; cross-platform; scenario reconstruction; ATT&CK mapping

Continued on next page

Table 1 – continued from previous page

Authors	Proposed Name	Objective	OS	Preprocessing	Model	Dataset	Results
Wei et al. (2022)	DeepHunter	Robust APT threat hunting via GNN-based graph pattern matching	Linux Windows	Provenance graph reduction; node attribute embedding using unsupervised NLP model (word2vec)	GNN-based graph pattern matching; attribute embedding network (attention); custom attention-based node embedding and GCN-based query graph embedding; NTN for similarity score	DARPA TC 3 scenarios, 2 synthetic scenarios	Detects all attack behaviors; high robustness to inconsistency/disconnection; outperforms Poirot and GNN baselines; near-zero false positives
Aly et al. (2024)	MEGR-APT	Scalable, memory-efficient APT hunting via attack-based subgraph matching	Linux FreeBSD Windows	RDF-based provenance graph, suspicious subgraph extraction (SPARQL), provenance graph reduction	GNN-based attack representation learning (RGCN) and global attention; NTN-based similarity;	DARPA TC3 8 scenarios (Linux, FreeBSD), OpTC 3 scenarios (Windows), real enterprise data	Detects all attacks; memory up to 2 orders of magnitude lower; comparable accuracy and speed; near-zero false positives
Milajerdi et al. (2021)	Poirot	Multi-stage APT detection using CTI-derived relationships and graph alignment	Linux Windows FreeBSD	Parse kernel audit logs; build provenance graph; extract and curate IOCs from CTI	Inexact graph pattern matching; influence score; seed-based alignment algorithm	DARPA TC: 10 scenarios, 7 public malware samples	Detects all attack scenarios; high accuracy; low false positives; robust to mutations; search in minutes; demonstrates that CTI correlations are robust and reliable for threat hunting
Hossain et al. (2018)	MORSE	Dependence explosion mitigation and robust APT scenario reconstruction via selective tag propagation	Linux FreeBSD	Parse kernel audit logs; build provenance graph; assign real-valued data and subject tags	Tag-based prioritization, attenuation and decay, conservative propagation, domain-specific event rules	DARPA TC3	11.4× fewer alarms; 35× smaller scenario graphs; detects stealthy, in-memory attacks; low memory use; milliseconds-level detection

Continued on next page

Table 1 – continued from previous page

Authors	Proposed Name	Objective	OS	Preprocessing	Model	Dataset	Results
Milajerdi et al. (2019)	HOLMES	Real-time, high-level APT detection and scenario summarization via correlated suspicious information flows	Linux FreeBSD Windows	Parse kernel audit logs, OS-neutral event normalization, provenance graph construction	TTP matching (MITRE ATT&CK), incremental scenario graph (HSG), noise reduction, severity-based ranking	DARPA TC: 9 scenarios	High precision and recall; low false positives; real-time compact scenario graphs; enterprise-scale deployment
Liu et al. (2021)	Log2vec	Detect insider threats and APTs at log-entry level in enterprise logs	Windows Linux	Heuristic rule-based construction of heterogeneous graphs from logs; meta-attribute parsing	Heterogeneous graph embedding (random walk and word2vec), clustering-based anomaly detection	CERT Insider Threat (5 scenarios, 6 malicious users), LANL (98 attackers)	Outperforms DeepLog, TIRESIAS, HMM in AUC and precision; effective for rare/fine-grained attacks; some false positives
Li et al. (2024)	ProvGRP	Context-aware provenance graph reduction and partitioning for efficient attack investigation	Linux Windows FreeBSD	Event similarity calculation (time interval, entity name, operation type); HDBSCAN clustering for process partitioning	Context-aware graph partitioning, behavior-unrelated event elimination, iterative path merging (improved Levenshtein distance)	ATLAS, DARPA CADETS	Up to 42.21× reduction, partition accuracy 0.805–0.954, preserves attack info, reduces investigation runtime by up to 61%
Wang et al. (2022)	ThreaTrace	Real-time, node-level host threat detection and tracing via provenance graph learning	Linux FreeBSD Windows	Streaming audit log collection; Camflow provenance graph; edge type distribution as node features; subgraph partitioning for memory efficiency	Semi-supervised anomaly detection; tailored GraphSAGE GNN; multi-model iterative training and prediction; waiting and tolerant thresholding for alerts	StreamSpot, Unicorn SC-1/SC-2, DARPA TC (5 datasets)	Outperforms Unicorn, ProvDetector, Log2vec in precision and recall; detects rare and stealthy threats early; scalable to long-term enterprise hosts

Continued on next page

Table 1 – continued from previous page

Authors	Proposed Name	Objective	OS	Preprocessing	Model	Dataset	Results
Zhu et al. (2023)	APT-SHIELD	Real-time APT detection, efficient attack chain analysis for Linux hosts	Linux	Auditd log collection, redundant semantics skipping, non-viable entity pruning	Custom rules-based label transfer and aggregation (MITRE ATT&CK-inspired)	Lab data (3 scenarios), DARPA Engagement (2 scenarios)	Detects diverse APTs (webshell, file-less, RAT); 20–35% data reduction; low false positives; stable memory overhead
Afnan et al. (2023)	LogShield	Transformer-based APT detection addressing scalability and feature extraction limits of deep learning	Windows Linux (DARPA OpTC and TC E3 datasets)	Event trace extraction from provenance graphs; log and temporal embedding; object-action and inter-event time encoding; downsampling for class balance	RoBERTa-based transformer model with self-attention; supervised cross-entropy loss	DARPA OpTC, DARPA TC E3	Outperforms LSTM/language models on long traces and large-scale data; reduces performance of short traces; higher memory/training cost
Alsaheel et al. (2021)	ATLAS	Automated attack story reconstruction from audit logs using causality analysis and sequence-based learning	Linux Windows (audit logs)	Lemmatized temporal sequence extraction; Levenshtein-based undersampling and mutation-based oversampling	LSTM-based sequence model with word embeddings; NLP preprocessing; supports multi-host investigation	Ten real-world APT scenarios (single- and multi-host testbed) [51]	Learns abstract attack strategies; requires true attack-symptom for each investigation; not robust to mimicry or false-positive triggers
Sun et al. (2023)	DEEPRO	APT campaign detection and attack entity identification using provenance graphs and metapath-based GNN	Windows (ATLAS dataset)	Provenance graph compression (merge duplicates, remove read-only and isolated nodes), Doc2vec-based node feature encoding	MAGNN with LeakyReLU and softmax for attention, weighted cross-entropy and supervised contrastive loss; process, file, and network entity correlation	ATLAS public dataset [51]	Improves detection and campaign reconstruction over rule-based and prior GNN methods; robust to graph heterogeneity; outperforms baseline methods in attack event pinpointing and campaign outline extraction

Continued on next page

Authors	Proposed Name	Objective	OS	Preprocessing	Model	Dataset	Results
Zhang et al. (2022)	KAIROS	Streaming, attack-agnostic, provenance-based intrusion detection and investigation	Linux (DARPA audit logs)	Hierarchical feature hashing, temporal windowing, node/edge featurization	Encoder-decoder graph learning, TGN encoder, MLP decoder, anomaly scoring (reconstruction error), Louvain community detection for summary graphs	DARPA E3, DARPA OpTC, Manzoor et al. dataset [52]	Accurately detects hidden and novel attacks; provides compact, actionable summaries; robust in large benign data; outperforms prior PIDS in scope, timeliness, and attack-agnostic detection
Sun et al. (2024)	ProcSAGE	Process-focused, host-based anomaly detection via an graph representation learning	Linux (host audit logs)	Provenance graph construction, subgraph extraction by syscall type, semantic (process name, syscall freq.) and topological (neighbor degree, clustering coeff.) features	GraphSAGE (mean aggregator, ReLU), iterative clustering (K-means-inspired), cross-entropy loss, fixed/relative outlier detection	Streamspot [52]	High accuracy and efficiency; robust to large audit volumes; outperforms prior provenance-based methods; no expert rules needed; may miss file/socket-only attacks; relies on audit granularity and windowing
Das et al. (2023)	Prov2vec	Continuous, unsupervised APT detection via compact provenance graph kernel representations	Linux Windows	Graph snapshotting, label-aware backward walks, causality-preserving duplicate elimination, node versioning, histosketch encoding	Provenance graph kernel; histosketch feature vectors; downstream, unsupervised, ML-based prediction tasks (graph classification, outlier detection, clustering)	DARPA OpTC; StreamSpot; Unicorn	Improved accuracy and efficiency over baselines; early APT detection; closed-world assumption; limited anomaly explainability (black-box ML)

Continued on next page

Table 1 – continued from previous page

Authors	Proposed Name	Objective	OS	Preprocessing	Model	Dataset	Results
Zhang et al. (2024)	APT-MGL	Self-supervised APT detection via masked graph representation learning and outlier detection	Linux audit logs	Log preprocessing; node type, degree, behavior (word2vec + temporal encoding); multi-head attention fusion	GraphMAE2 masked self-encoder, GAT decoder, KNN outlier detection	DARPA TC-E3; StreamSpot	High accuracy and efficiency; adapts to new benign data; low computational cost; closed-world assumption; attack localization only, no attack classification
Jiang et al.	RT-APT	Real-time anomaly detection for APTs on large-scale provenance graphs	Linux	SPADE-based log collection; FlexSketch for feature vectorization and concept drift	WL subtree kernel, FlexSketch for streaming summarization and handling concept drift, K-means clustering	StreamSpot, Unicorn, RT-APT Laboratory datasets	Outperforms SOTA in runtime, memory, CPU; detects novel behaviors and abnormal transitions; assumes secure initial modeling; may have false positives on unseen benign activity; parameter tuning required
Wang et al.	-	APT attack detection using a knowledge graph of vulnerabilities, weaknesses, and attack methods with GCNs (based on threat intelligence sources)	Linux Windows	Text cleaning and tokenization of CVE descriptions, feature extraction using bag-of-words and vocabulary building, convert heterogeneous sources to homogeneous graph	GCN applied to homogeneous graph; ReLU for propagation, softmax for classification	12 APT scenarios	Detects APTs via vulnerability relationships; loss of info from graph simplification; lacks adaptive updating; proposes heterogeneous GNNs and adaptive models as future work
Xiao et al. (2024)	APT-MMF	APT actor attribution using heterogeneous CTI and multimodal feature fusion	Not specified	Entity extraction, graph construction, feature encoding (BERT, Node2vec, ordinal/ID encoding)	Multilevel heterogeneous graph attention networks (IOC type-level, metapath-based, semantic-level)	1300 APT reports (21 groups) from multisource CTI	High attribution accuracy and robustness; interpretable; future work targets sociopolitical features and unknown actor support

Continued on next page

Table 1 – continued from previous page

Authors	Proposed Name	Objective	OS	Preprocessing	Model	Dataset	Results
Akar and Selvi (2024)	APT-Scope	APT group prediction and alias discovery from enriched CTI graphs	Not specified	NER, regex-based IoC extraction, passive and active CTI enrichment	FastRP embedding, Logistic Regression, Random Forest, MLP	783 APT reports and malware data from OSINT	Discovers hidden group links and actors; scalable CTI enrichment; future work includes more entity types and predictive NER
Shenderovitz and Nissim (2024)	Bon-APT	APT detection, attribution, and explainability via temporal segmentation of API calls	Windows	Cuckoo sandbox execution, dynamic API trace capture, segment-wise aggregation	Temporal segmentation, API abstraction, Random Forest, LSTM, MLP	121,513 PE files (12,655 APTs, 188 groups, 17 nations)	Strong detection and attribution; interpretable behavior segments; future work targets deep temporal models and filtering routine behavior
Coulter et al. (2024)	-	APT detection via transfer learning and file system log adaptation	Windows	Log pre-processing, temporal filtering, geodesics projection, APT-BN modeling	Domain adaptation (geodesic mapping), APT-BN, SVM, RF, Log2Vec	APT-EXE, target dataset(183 APT samples + benign data)	Outperforms TFidf and embeddings; low false positives; adaptable to unseen APT logs; future work includes adaptive tuning and network log integration

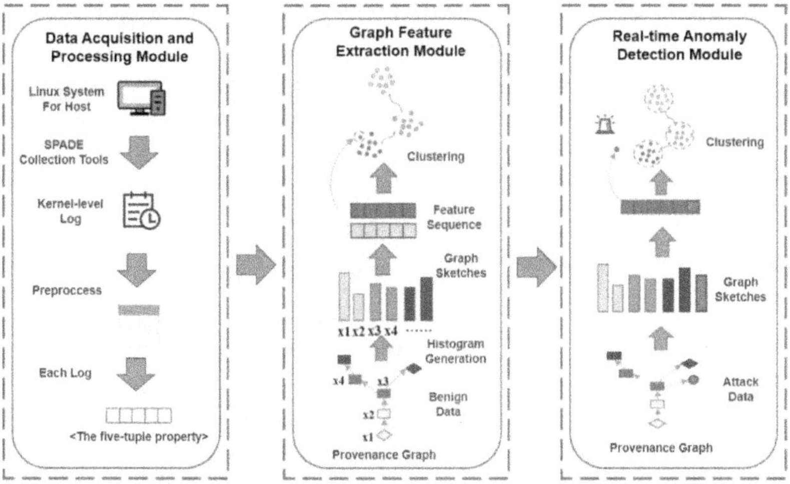

Figure 30: RT-APT architecture: kernel log collection (SPADE), WL subtree kernel embedding, FlexSketch vectorization and concept drift adaptation, and K-means anomaly detection [25].

2.4 Synthesis

Despite significant advancements in Advanced Persistent Threat (APT) detection methodologies, several fundamental gaps that limit their effectiveness in real-world applications persist. The most critical issues identified in the literature include:

- **Outdated and Limited APT Datasets for Training and Evaluation:**
  - Many datasets commonly used for APT detection are several years old and no longer reflect the diverse tactics, techniques, and procedures (TTPs) of modern threat actors.
  - Some datasets focus on particular scenarios, such as Linux-only environments, and do not cover the full range of operating systems, platforms, and attack surfaces seen in real incidents.
  - Because real-world enterprise telemetry is often proprietary and operating systems are closed-source, obtaining relevant and up-to-date data is challenging.
  - Several datasets are generated from lab-controlled, self-designed attacks based on the researchers' own infrastructure. While useful for testing, these attacks may not mirror the complexity, stealth, or multi-stage coordination of real-world, known APT campaigns.
  - The lack of large, labeled, and multi-modal datasets, which include logs, network traces, binaries, and memory data, limits the potential of data-driven detection models.
- **Absence of an End-to-End APT Detection Framework:**
  - Many existing solutions detect isolated malicious events, such as a single process execution or network connection, without connecting them to the broader campaign they belong to.
  - APT campaigns involve multiple, coordinated phases (reconnaissance, compromise, privilege escalation, lateral movement, persistence, and exfiltration) that must be correlated to reveal the complete attack chain.
  - A comprehensive detection model must identify malicious entities and reconstruct the complete attack scenario to understand the sequence, causality, and scope of the intrusion.
  - Current approaches rarely integrate heterogeneous data sources (system logs, network flows, endpoint telemetry) into a unified view, resulting in fragmented and context-poor detections.
  - Few frameworks incorporate temporal and causal analysis to determine the order of events, which is useful for differentiating between legitimate sequences of activity and malicious chains of actions.
- **Challenges in APT Group Attribution:**
  - According to existing studies, there is no non-rule-based published work that directly links a detected attack to a specific, known APT group.
  - Most current approaches focus solely on detecting the occurrence of an APT attack, without attributing it to a particular threat actor.

  - Attribution can provide valuable intelligence regarding the likely origin of the attack, the attacker's motivations, and their potential future actions.
  - Effective attribution requires not only detecting malicious activity but also understanding the contextual patterns, behaviors, and tactics characteristic of specific APT groups.
  - Data-driven methods, such as machine learning models trained on labeled historical attack data, can be used to automate this attribution process and reduce reliance on manual analyst expertise.

- **Scalability and Real-Time Processing Limitations in Provenance Graph Analysis:**
  - Provenance-based detection can be extremely resource-intensive, especially as the number of nodes and edges grows into the millions in enterprise environments.
  - The vast number of nodes and edges involved in system-level interactions necessitates efficient methods for storing, querying, and analyzing provenance graphs.
  - Many existing approaches process entire graphs in memory, which is impractical for continuous, real-time monitoring at scale.
  - Without scalable, incremental, or streaming-based graph processing techniques, detection delays increase significantly, reducing the ability to respond to threats in time.

- **Accuracy Challenges and High False Positive Rates:**
  - Many detection models either trigger too many false alerts or miss subtle, stealthy threats.
  - Excessive false positives can overwhelm security analysts, leading to alert fatigue and the possibility of missing genuine threats.
  - Striking the right balance between sensitivity and precision remains an ongoing challenge.

- **Inefficiencies of Anomaly Detection Models:**
  - Anomaly detection models frequently fail to distinguish between unusual but benign activities and genuine attacks, leading to a high rate of false positives.
  - These models often fail to learn from attack behaviors, thereby limiting their ability to adapt to evolving threats.
  - The inability to attribute detected anomalies to known APT activities further complicates incident response efforts.

- **Limitations of Rule-Based Models:**
  - Models that rely solely on predefined rules for detecting malicious sequences are susceptible to evasion techniques and can be bypassed with small changes to an attack's execution.
  - The static nature of rule-based models limits their adaptability to new attack vectors and tactics employed by adversaries.

- **Limited Use of Multi-Source Telemetry:**

- Many detection systems operate on a single data type (such as system logs), ignoring valuable context from network data, endpoint monitoring, and external threat intelligence feeds.
- Without this fusion of sources, important links between different stages of an attack can be missed, resulting in incomplete detection and analysis.
- However, managing the scalability and computational cost of processing and correlating such large volumes of information remains a major challenge.

In summary, while the research community has made significant strides in APT detection, progress is still needed in several areas: building diverse and regularly updated datasets; designing end-to-end frameworks that connect all stages of an attack; improving scalability and real-time graph analysis; enabling accurate and automated attribution; integrating multiple telemetry sources; and making models more transparent and analyst-friendly. Addressing these points will lead to more precise, actionable, and resilient detection systems that can keep pace with the evolving nature of APT campaigns.

Building on these observations, the model proposed in this thesis explicitly addresses several of the challenges highlighted above. By generating a new dataset of multi-day, multi-host APT campaigns, the work contributes more realistic training and evaluation data. The framework integrates heterogeneous node feature encoding, malicious node detection, malicious subgraph extraction, and APT group attribution into a unified pipeline, thereby closing the gap between isolated detections and end-to-end campaign analysis. Scalability concerns are mitigated through neighborhood sampling, dropout-based graph augmentation, and gradient accumulation, enabling efficient learning on provenance graphs with millions of nodes. While the malicious node detection model may still raise false alarms, these are substantially reduced in the attribution stage, where the interactions among malicious nodes are analyzed and campaign-level behaviors can be distinguished from benign activity. Furthermore, the dataset and framework incorporate multiple sources of telemetry, including not only system-level logs such as processes, files, and registry modifications, but also network connections, which allows for a richer and more comprehensive view of attack behavior. Finally, the combination of edge-aware attention, residual connections, and weighted loss functions directly tackles the imbalance between benign and malicious nodes, improving both accuracy and interpretability. Together, these design choices make the proposed framework better aligned with real-world requirements for detecting and attributing APT activity.

3 Methodology

3.1 Background of Graph Neural Networks

In the context of Advanced Persistent Threat (APT) detection, particularly in provenance-based attack detection systems, large-scale dynamic graphs are often used to model the behavior of attackers. These graphs, which represent the complex interactions between various system entities (e.g., processes, files, users, etc.), contain millions of nodes and edges, often with heterogeneous types. Directly applying traditional Graph Neural Network (GNN) training methods to such graphs is computationally prohibitive. Given the high number of node and edge types, a proper GNN architecture must be selected that can effectively learn the attack-related information and structural patterns within these large and heterogeneous graphs.
After a comprehensive review of the GNN literature, the following subsections present key models and training strategies that are most relevant for attack detection on provenance graphs. We begin by outlining foundational architectures such as GCN, GAT, and GraphSAGE. Each subsection highlights how the model operates, its main advantages and limitations, and its suitability for large, dynamic, and heterogeneous graphs encountered in APT detection.

3.1.1 Inductive and Transductive Learning

GNNs can be trained using two paradigms: inductive and transductive learning. The choice between these two depends on whether the model needs to generalize to new, unseen nodes or if it will only operate on the nodes seen during training.

- **Inductive Learning:** In inductive learning, the model is trained using a subset of nodes and tested on unseen nodes. The learned representations can generalize to new, unseen nodes or graphs. This is particularly useful for real-time attack detection, where new attack patterns and unknown nodes appear frequently. The goal is to learn a function $f(\mathbf{X})$ that maps from node features to labels, generalizing well across unseen nodes.

$$h_u = f(\mathbf{X_u}, \theta)$$

  where h_u is the embedding of an unseen node u, and $\mathbf{X_u}$ is its feature vector.

- **Transductive Learning:** In transductive learning, the model is trained and tested on the same set of nodes. The goal is to predict the labels for all the nodes in the graph, assuming the graph structure is fixed. This approach does not generalize well to new, unseen nodes but is useful when working with fixed datasets.

$$h_i = f(\mathbf{X_i}, \mathbf{A}, \theta)$$

  where h_i is the embedding of node i, $\mathbf{A}$ is the adjacency matrix, and θ represents the learned parameters of the model.

Inductive learning is preferred in APT detection, as it allows the model to adapt to new attack vectors and dynamically evolving graphs, where nodes (such as new processes or users) are continuously added. Conversely, transductive learning is better suited for tasks where the graph structure is fixed, and there is no need for the model to generalize beyond the seen nodes.

3.1.2 Full-Batch, Stochastic, and Mini-Batch Gradient Descent

The first step in selecting the appropriate training paradigm is to evaluate the typical gradient descent strategies employed in GNNs. Given the scale and nature of attack graphs, both full-batch and stochastic gradient descent (SGD) were found to be infeasible for this use case:

- **Full-Batch Gradient Descent** is not suitable for large-scale graphs because it requires processing the entire graph at once. This results in extremely high memory usage and computational overhead, making it impractical for dynamic attack graphs that frequently change and contain millions of nodes and edges.
- **Stochastic Gradient Descent (SGD)** updates the model based on a single randomly chosen node per iteration. While memory-efficient, this approach is computationally inefficient for large graphs as it leads to slow convergence due to noisy gradients, and fails to capture the global structural patterns across large subgraphs, which is crucial for attack detection.
- **Mini-Batch Gradient Descent** offers a balanced approach by dividing the graph into smaller, manageable batches. This method allows for frequent updates and is computationally efficient. However, it heavily depends on how the mini-batches are sampled to ensure that the graph's structural information is preserved while reducing computational overhead.

Mini-batch gradient descent, in combination with appropriate sampling techniques, is selected as the most suitable option for attack detection tasks on large-scale provenance graphs.

3.1.3 Batch Sampling

Training on full provenance graphs is infeasible, so mini-batches must be constructed to balance efficiency with structural fidelity. The sampling scheme determines each node's receptive field and directly affects convergence, stability, and recall of rare malicious patterns. We review node sampling, layer sampling, and subgraph sampling, outlining how each trades memory and speed against the preservation of local context that is essential for accurate APT detection.

3.1.3.1 Node Sampling

Node sampling is a commonly used technique to define mini-batches in GNNs, particularly in GraphSAGE [53]. This method involves randomly selecting a subset of target nodes and recursively sampling a fixed number of neighbors from each layer, which forms the receptive field for each node. Importantly, GraphSAGE utilizes random neighborhood sampling to gather neighbors, making it an efficient choice for large-scale graphs.

The procedure for node sampling involves the following steps:

1. Randomly define mini-batches of seed nodes.

2. For each selected node, recursively sample a fixed number of neighbors from each layer in the graph until the receptive field reaches the desired size.

3. Aggregate the layers and neighbors of each node to update node embeddings.

Advantages:

- Reduces the memory footprint by processing only a subset of the graph.

- Enables the model to scale to large graphs containing millions of nodes, which is common in APT detection tasks.

- Random neighborhood sampling in GraphSAGE helps prevent overfitting by ensuring a random and varied training process.

Disadvantages:

- *Redundant computation:* Because neighbors of different nodes may overlap, the embeddings of shared neighbors must be recomputed multiple times, leading to inefficiency.

- The random selection of neighbors may sometimes result in non-optimal subgraphs, potentially missing important attack patterns present in distant or less connected nodes.

For this research, node sampling is the most practical choice due to the focus on node classification. This task only requires information from the neighborhood of each node rather than the global context of the graph. Additionally, node sampling offers better scalability and efficiency, particularly when dealing with imbalanced datasets, a common characteristic of attack detection scenarios.
Given these advantages, we adopt a customized node sampling strategy that accounts for the weaknesses of this method as well as the class imbalance in the dataset. This ensures that underrepresented classes are adequately sampled, allowing the model to learn attack-related patterns more effectively. The details of this strategy are provided in Section 3.2.5.

3.1.3.2 Layer Sampling

Layer sampling techniques, used in FastGCN [54] and LADIES [55], improve upon node sampling by addressing the redundancy issue. In layer sampling, nodes are sampled independently for each layer, reducing overlap and ensuring that computations at each layer are more efficient.
The process of layer sampling involves the following steps:

1. In the FastGCN approach, calculate node sampling probabilities based on their degree. This determines how many neighbors each node should sample.

2. Independently sample a fixed number of nodes for each layer using these computed probabilities.

3. The sampled nodes from each layer are aggregated, and a smaller adjacency matrix is constructed for efficient computation.

4. LADIES further improves the process by constructing a bipartite graph between adjacent layers, where nodes' sampling probabilities are adjusted based on their importance in the network.

Advantages:

- Reduces redundant computations across layers.
- Improves memory usage and computational efficiency compared to node sampling.
- Helps avoid the explosive growth of the receptive field as the graph deepens.

Disadvantages:

- May disrupt the graph's local structure, as nodes in consecutive layers are sampled independently, potentially resulting in isolated or disconnected nodes.
- The disruption of local structure can impact performance in tasks where structural dependencies between layers are crucial.

3.1.3.3 Subgraph Sampling

Subgraph sampling methods, such as ClusterGCN [56] and GraphSAINT [57], partition the graph into disjoint subgraphs or clusters. These clusters are then treated as independent mini-batches, significantly improving the scalability of the GNN model. Subgraph sampling helps ensure that the model can efficiently process massive graphs by reducing the number of nodes and edges involved in each training step.
However, despite its scalability, subgraph sampling has a significant limitation in terms of computational cost and complexity. Given the high overhead associated with clustering, and the fact that node classification relies only on local neighborhood information rather than global structure, subgraph sampling is not the optimal choice for this use case. Instead, node sampling proves to be a more efficient and cost-effective approach, especially the customized algorithm we used to address class imbalance.

3.1.4 Graph Neural Networks for Attack Detection

In the context of Advanced Persistent Threat (APT) detection, particularly in provenance-based attack detection systems, large-scale dynamic graphs are used to model the behavior of attackers. These graphs, which represent the interactions between various system entities (e.g., processes, files, users), contain millions of nodes and edges, often with heterogeneous types. Graph Neural Networks (GNNs) provide a framework to learn meaningful representations of these entities by iteratively aggregating information from their local neighborhoods. Directly applying traditional Graph Neural Network (GNN) training methods to such graphs is computationally prohibitive. Given the high number of node and edge types, it is essential to choose a GNN architecture that can effectively learn attack-related patterns and structural dependencies in large and heterogeneous graphs.

This section discusses several popular GNN models, their general working principles, and their suitability for APT detection. The models presented here include the General GNN framework, Graph Convolutional Networks (GCN), Graph Attention Networks (GAT), GraphSAGE, ClusterGCN, and GraphSAINT. Each model has its unique features that can be leveraged depending on the characteristics of the attack graph, such as its size, complexity, and the task at hand.

3.1.4.1 General GNN Framework.

Let $G = (V, E)$ be a graph with node set V and edge set E. Each node $v \in V$ is associated with an initial feature vector $\mathbf{h}_v^{(0)} \in \mathbb{R}^d$. A generic GNN layer updates the node embeddings as:

$$\mathbf{h}_v^{(k)} = \text{UPDATE}^{(k)}\left(\mathbf{h}_v^{(k-1)},\ \text{AGGREGATE}^{(k)}\left(\{\mathbf{h}_u^{(k-1)} : u \in \mathcal{N}(v)\}\right)\right),$$

where:

- $\mathbf{h}_v^{(k)}$ is the embedding of node v at the k-th layer.
- $\mathcal{N}(v)$ denotes the set of neighbors of node v.
- $\text{AGGREGATE}^{(k)}$ is a permutation-invariant function (e.g., sum, mean, attention) that combines neighbor embeddings.
- $\text{UPDATE}^{(k)}$ is a learnable transformation (often a linear layer followed by a non-linearity).

After K layers, the final embedding $\mathbf{h}_v^{(K)}$ integrates both node attributes and multi-hop structural information. These embeddings can then be used for downstream tasks such as node classification, link prediction, or detecting malicious entities in provenance graphs.

3.1.4.2 Graph Convolutional Networks (GCN).

GCNs extend the general GNN by defining aggregation as a normalized sum of neighbor features. In matrix form:

$$\mathbf{H}^{(k)} = \sigma\left(\hat{D}^{-\frac{1}{2}}\hat{A}\hat{D}^{-\frac{1}{2}}\mathbf{H}^{(k-1)}W^{(k)}\right),$$

where $\hat{A} = A + I$ is the adjacency matrix with self-loops and $\hat{D}$ is its degree matrix.
Key Characteristics:

- Aggregation via spectral graph convolutions based on the graph Laplacian.
- Layer-wise propagation with normalized neighbor averaging.
- Each node's representation is updated through a weighted sum of neighbor features.

Applications:

- Node classification.

- Link prediction.
- Graph-level classification.

Limitations:

- Over-smoothing: deeper layers lead to indistinguishable embeddings across nodes.
- Scalability: computing and storing normalized adjacency is costly for large provenance graphs.

3.1.4.3 Graph Attention Networks (GAT).

Graph Attention Networks (GAT) extend the general GNN framework by introducing an attention mechanism that dynamically weighs the importance of neighbors when updating node representations. Unlike GCN, which treats all neighbors equally after normalization, GAT computes learnable attention scores that adapt to the context of each node and its neighbors.

Each node v starts with an input feature vector $\mathbf{h}_v^{(k-1)}$, which is linearly transformed using a weight matrix W. For every neighbor $u \in \mathcal{N}(v)$, an attention coefficient is first computed:

$$e_{vu} = \text{LeakyReLU}\left(\mathbf{a}^\top \left[W\mathbf{h}_v^{(k-1)} \parallel W\mathbf{h}_u^{(k-1)}\right]\right),$$

where $\mathbf{a}$ is a learnable attention vector and $\parallel$ denotes concatenation. These raw scores are then normalized across all neighbors of v using a softmax function:

$$\alpha_{vu} = \frac{\exp(e_{vu})}{\sum_{u' \in \mathcal{N}(v)} \exp(e_{vu'})},$$

so that $\sum_{u \in \mathcal{N}(v)} \alpha_{vu} = 1$. The final node representation is obtained as:

$$\mathbf{h}_v^{(k)} = \sigma\left(\sum_{u \in \mathcal{N}(v)} \alpha_{vu} W\mathbf{h}_u^{(k-1)}\right),$$

where σ is a non-linear activation (e.g., ReLU or ELU). This formulation ensures that more relevant neighbors (e.g., processes exhibiting suspicious interactions) have higher weights in the aggregation.

To improve stability and expressiveness, GAT employs **multi-head attention**, where multiple independent attention mechanisms are applied in parallel. Their outputs are either concatenated or averaged:

$$\mathbf{h}_v^{(k)} = \Big\Vert_{m=1}^{M} \sigma\left(\sum_{u \in \mathcal{N}(v)} \alpha_{vu}^{(m)} W^{(m)} \mathbf{h}_u^{(k-1)}\right),$$

where M is the number of attention heads. Concatenation is typically used for intermediate layers, while averaging is used for the final layer to stabilize the output.

Key Characteristics:

- Learns attention weights that adaptively highlight the most important neighbors.
- Multi-head attention captures diverse patterns and improves training stability.

- Inductive capability: can generalize to unseen nodes and evolving graphs.
- GAT does not require the full graph structure upfront, allowing for more flexible graph processing and reducing the computational overhead.
- GAT can handle graphs with varying node degrees and does not require the graph to be undirected
- GAT does not require matrix inversion or expensive spectral operations. It is parallelizable across nodes and edges, making it computationally efficient.

Applications:

- Node classification in dynamic graphs.
- Situations where not all neighbors are equally relevant, such as APT detection, where a few anomalous interactions should dominate the decision.
- Graphs with heterogeneous degrees, where fixed normalization is insufficient.

Limitations:

- Higher computational and memory cost due to multi-head attention.

3.1.4.4 GraphSAGE: Inductive Representation Learning on Large Graphs.

GraphSAGE (Graph Sample and Aggregation) is designed for inductive learning on large and evolving graphs. Unlike transductive approaches such as GCN, which assume the full graph is available during training, GraphSAGE can generalize to unseen nodes and subgraphs. This inductive capability makes it particularly valuable for APT detection, where new processes, files, or network connections frequently appear.

The core idea of GraphSAGE is to learn node embeddings by sampling and aggregating information from a fixed number of neighbors, rather than using all neighbors. This makes the model scalable to large graphs while retaining expressive power.

At each layer k, the neighborhood of a node v is first sampled, and the features of these neighbors are aggregated:

$$\mathbf{h}_{\mathcal{N}(v)}^{(k)} = \text{AGGREGATE}^{(k)}\left(\{\mathbf{h}_u^{(k-1)} : u \in \mathcal{N}(v)\}\right),$$

where $\mathbf{h}_{\mathcal{N}(v)}^{(k)}$ represents the aggregated embedding of the sampled neighbors of v. The aggregation function can vary:

- **Mean Aggregator:** takes the element-wise mean of neighbors.
- **Pooling Aggregator:** applies a non-linear function (e.g., max pooling) after a transformation.
- **LSTM Aggregator:** processes neighbors sequentially with an LSTM to capture order-sensitive dependencies.

The node v's representation is then updated by concatenating its own embedding with the aggregated neighborhood embedding and applying a transformation:

$$\mathbf{h}_v^{(k)} = \sigma\Big(W^{(k)} \cdot \big[\mathbf{h}_v^{(k-1)} \,\|\, \mathbf{h}_{\mathcal{N}(v)}^{(k)}\big]\Big),$$

where $W^{(k)}$ is a learnable weight matrix, $\|$ denotes concatenation, and σ is a non-linear activation function. This formulation ensures that the updated embedding of each node depends both on its previous embedding and on aggregated neighbor information.

For unsupervised training, GraphSAGE often employs a graph-based loss that encourages similar embeddings for connected nodes and dissimilar embeddings for non-connected nodes:

$$\mathcal{L} = -\sum_{(i,j)\in E} \log(\sigma(\mathbf{h}_i^\top \mathbf{h}_j)) - \sum_{(i,k)\in \mathrm{Neg}(i)} \log(1 - \sigma(\mathbf{h}_i^\top \mathbf{h}_k)),$$

where E is the set of edges, σ is the sigmoid function, and $\mathrm{Neg}(i)$ is a set of negative samples not connected to i. This objective enables GraphSAGE to learn embeddings that preserve local graph structures without relying on node labels.

Key Characteristics:

- **Inductive capability:** can embed previously unseen nodes during inference.
- **Neighborhood sampling:** limits the number of neighbors, enabling training on huge graphs.
- **Flexible aggregation:** supports multiple aggregation strategies (mean, pooling, LSTM).

Applications:

- Real-time APT detection, where new nodes (processes, files, users) continuously emerge.
- Large-scale node classification tasks on evolving graphs.
- Embedding heterogeneous system audit logs for downstream detection and attribution.

Limitations:

- Random sampling may omit critical neighbors, causing loss of important attack-related patterns.
- Embedding quality depends strongly on the choice of aggregator (e.g., mean aggregator may fail to capture complex dependencies).
- May require careful hyperparameter tuning to balance efficiency and representation richness.

3.1.4.5 GraphSAINT: Graph Sampling-Based Inductive Learning.

GraphSAINT (Graph Sampling-Based Inductive Learning) is designed to scale GNN training to huge graphs by sampling *subgraphs* instead of full neighborhoods. This allows the model to capture higher-order structures while reducing memory and computation costs, which is especially useful for provenance graphs with millions of nodes.

At each iteration, a subgraph $G_s = (V_s, E_s) \subseteq G$ is sampled, and updates are performed only on G_s. The propagation rule follows the general GNN framework:

$$\mathbf{h}_v^{(k)} = \text{UPDATE}^{(k)}\left(\mathbf{h}_v^{(k-1)},\ \text{AGGREGATE}^{(k)}\left(\{\mathbf{h}_u^{(k-1)} : u \in \mathcal{N}_{G_s}(v)\}\right)\right),$$

where $\mathcal{N}_{G_s}(v)$ is the neighborhood of v restricted to the sampled subgraph. To correct for biased sampling, each sampled node v with probability q_v is re-weighted in the loss:

$$\mathcal{L} = \sum_{v \in V_s} \frac{1}{q_v} \cdot \ell\left(\mathbf{h}_v^{(K)}, y_v\right).$$

Sampling Strategies: GraphSAINT supports several sampling methods:

- **Node sampling:** select a set of nodes uniformly and use their induced subgraph.
- **Edge sampling:** sample edges and include their endpoints, favoring highly connected regions.
- **Random walk sampling:** build subgraphs by simulating short random walks, which better preserve local connectivity.

These strategies strike a balance between efficiency and representational fidelity, but the choice of method significantly impacts the model's effectiveness.

Key Characteristics:

- Subgraph-level sampling reduces computation while retaining local structures.
- Importance re-weighting preserves unbiasedness of gradient estimates.
- Inductive learning capability similar to GraphSAGE.

Applications:

- Large-scale node and graph classification.
- Web-scale graphs where full-batch training is infeasible.
- Provenance-based APT detection with dense audit logs.

Limitations:

- Model performance is sensitive to the choice of sampling strategy; poor sampling can miss rare but critical attack paths.
- Subgraph construction introduces preprocessing and runtime complexity.
- Neighborhood sizes are inconsistent across nodes due to subgraph sampling, which can degrade accuracy for node classification tasks where uniform receptive fields are important.
- Training is less stable compared to neighbor-sampling methods like GraphSAGE, especially on highly dynamic or sparse graphs.
- Importance re-weighting may lead to high variance in gradient estimates, slowing convergence.

3.1.4.6 Conclusion

Among the presented GNN models, GCN, GraphSAGE, and GAT share a common foundation of neighborhood aggregation; however, they differ significantly in terms of scalability and flexibility. GCNs, while conceptually simple and effective for small to medium graphs, are limited by their dependence on the full adjacency matrix and susceptibility to over-smoothing, making them less suitable for large provenance graphs with millions of nodes. ClusterGCN and GraphSAINT improve scalability through partitioning or subgraph sampling; however, they introduce variability in neighborhood size and training stability, which can hinder performance in fine-grained node classification tasks, such as identifying malicious processes.
In contrast, GraphSAGE and GAT address the specific challenges posed by provenance-based APT detection more effectively:

- **GraphSAGE** offers scalability through fixed-size neighborhood sampling, which ensures consistent receptive fields across nodes. This property is crucial for node classification tasks where embeddings must be comparable. Moreover, its inductive capability allows embeddings to be generated for new processes, files, or users as they appear, a common scenario in dynamic system monitoring.

- **GAT** enhances expressiveness by applying attention mechanisms that learn the relative importance of neighbors. This is particularly valuable in provenance graphs, where most neighbors represent benign activity and only a few edges (e.g., rare file accesses or unusual process interactions) indicate malicious behavior. By assigning higher weights to these critical neighbors, GAT helps focus the model on the most relevant structures.

3.2 Proposed Model

In this work, we propose **EAGLE-APT**. This provenance-based APT detection framework leverages heterogeneous provenance graphs and Graph Neural Networks (GNNs) to detect and attribute advanced persistent attacks. The framework follows a multi-stage workflow, illustrated in Figure 31, which integrates data collection, graph construction, node-level detection, subgraph extraction, and APT attribution. At a high level, the main stages are:

- **Log Collection and Preprocessing:** Windows event logs from multiple channels, including Sysmon, Security, Application, Background Intelligent Transfer Service (BITS), and Task Scheduler, are collected and parsed to capture diverse system activities such as process, file, registry, DLL, driver, scheduled task, and network events.

- **Provenance Graph Generation:** From the processed logs, a heterogeneous provenance graph is constructed. The graph represents system entities as nodes and their interactions as typed edges, encoding causal and temporal relationships among events.

- **Node Feature Extraction:** Semantic and structural features are extracted separately for each node type, ensuring that rich, type-specific attributes represent heterogeneous entities.

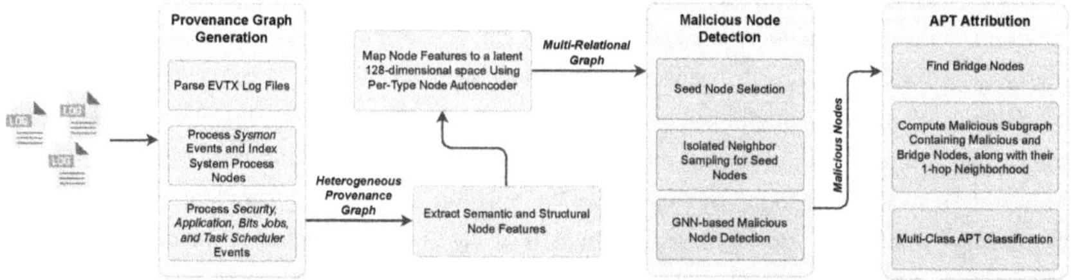

Figure 31: Overall architecture of the proposed EAGLE-APT framework. The pipeline integrates provenance graph construction, node feature extraction, embedding, malicious node detection, malicious subgraph extraction, and APT group attribution.

- **Node Embedding:** Extracted features are mapped into a shared 128-dimensional latent space using per-type autoencoders. This aligns heterogeneous node attributes into a unified embedding format suitable for downstream graph learning while retaining type-aware distinctions.

- **Seed Node Selection and Sampling:** Candidate seed nodes are selected, and neighborhood sampling is applied to scale training to large graphs. Each batch is constructed to contain 20% malicious nodes, ensuring that rare positive samples are adequately represented despite their natural scarcity.

- **Malicious Node Detection:** A hybrid GNN model composed of a GraphSAGE layer and an edge-aware GAT layer with residual connections classifies nodes as benign or malicious. This stage provides fine-grained detection of compromised entities.

- **Bridge Node Selection and Malicious Subgraph Extraction:** From the detected malicious nodes, bridge nodes are identified within their two-hop neighborhoods, and the full one-hop neighborhood of the combined set is extracted. This results in malicious subgraphs that capture both compromised entities and their surrounding context.

- **APT Attribution:** Malicious subgraphs are aggregated into graph-level embeddings using attention-based pooling and classified into known APT groups through a multi-class GNN classifier. This stage mitigates potential false alarms raised by the malicious node detector by considering the broader interactions of malicious nodes and distinguishing coordinated attack behavior from benign activity.

Together, these stages form an end-to-end workflow that moves from raw system logs to high-level attribution. By unifying heterogeneous data, detecting malicious entities, reconstructing their interactions, and linking them to specific APT groups, the framework provides both fine-grained detection and actionable threat intelligence.

3.2.1 Heterogeneous Provenance Graph Construction

Provenance-based analysis has emerged as a dominant paradigm in recent research on APT and advanced malware detection, as evidenced in the literature review section. However, through our survey of existing approaches, we observe that the full expressive potential of provenance graphs has not been fully realized in any prior work. Most published methods simplify the system model by restricting node types to only processes, files, and (occasionally) network connections, with very limited or coarse-grained relationships among them. While such simplifications aid tractability and reduce the complexity of downstream graph learning, they also result in substantial information loss. For instance, details about registry modifications, scheduled task creation, BITS job management, DLL side-loading, and pipe-based inter-process communication, each of which are frequently leveraged by APT actors to evade detection or maintain persistence, are either omitted or collapsed into generic activity categories. As a result, subtle attack chains involving these techniques may remain undetected.

It is also recognized that not all details from operating system logs can be directly or meaningfully mapped into a graph structure. For example, specific fields (such as full memory dumps, environment variables, or verbose textual descriptions) are either impractical to encode as graph attributes or would introduce excessive noise and dimensionality into the learning process. Nonetheless, by adopting a more comprehensive schema that includes additional system entities, such as registry keys, scheduled tasks, BITS jobs, DLLs, drivers, devices, domains, and named pipes, and a richer set of edge types, we can preserve a much larger fraction of the behavioral information present in the original logs. For example, our generated graphs can capture the use of scheduled tasks for establishing persistence or lateral movement, registry key manipulations for stealthy configuration changes, BITS job abuse for covert file transfer, DLL side-loading for privilege escalation, and the creation and use of named pipes for C2 and lateral communications.

To achieve this, during dataset generation and graph construction, we iteratively examined all available event types produced in our dataset, manually investigating their semantics and information content. We then extended our graph generation code to integrate all events that encode meaningful system behaviors, while discarding those that cannot be robustly represented or would not contribute to attack chain reconstruction. This process led to the identification and inclusion of 38 informative event types spanning the Sysmon, Security, Application, BITS, and TaskScheduler sources, as detailed in the following sections.

3.2.1.1 Workflow:

The construction of the provenance graph proceeds as follows:

1. **Experiment timeline acquisition:** For each attack day, the relevant time window is extracted from the `timeline.txt` file, providing the precise bounds for analysis and ensuring temporal consistency across logs.

2. **EVTX log enumeration and parsing:** All available EVTX log files (*e.g.*, Sysmon, Security, Application, System, TaskScheduler, BITS) for each machine are identified and loaded using the open-source `PyEvtxParser` library.

3. **Sysmon-first process tracking:** Windows Sysmon logs serve as the main authoritative source for process objects in the provenance graph. Sysmon uniquely identifies each process with a globally unique process GUID, and includes detailed parent/child process relationships, creation and termination times, and command-line information. To ensure consistent entity tracking, all Sysmon EVTX

files are parsed *prior* to other log sources, constructing a comprehensive index of process lifetimes. For events from other log sources, such as Security or Application, processes are matched to Sysmon-derived nodes via a triple of process ID, process image name, and event timestamp, using the indexed process lifetimes to resolve ambiguities and track even short-lived processes. This cross-log correlation ensures every graph node reflects a unique system entity. This step forms the backbone of process identity resolution for the entire graph.

4. **Processing remaining log sources:** After Sysmon, the rest of the EVTX sources (Security, Application, BITS, TaskScheduler, etc.) are parsed. For each event referencing a process, a matching process node is found by comparing process ID, image name, and timestamp against the Sysmon-derived process lifetime index. This enables unambiguous mapping of all activities to unique process entities, even in the presence of PID reuse and process short lifetimes.

5. **Event deduplication and coverage analysis:** Because the dataset's log files can overlap due to log collection intervals, every event is identified by its `EventRecordID` (unique per machine and log source) and timestamp. Before processing any event, the tuple `(EventRecordID, timestamp)` is checked against a per-machine and per-source lookup table to ensure that each event is included in the graph at most once. This guarantees both accuracy and reproducibility in the resulting graph.

6. **Event ID whitelisting and comprehensive graph coverage:** To ensure maximal information extraction, a running list of unused event IDs (those not covered by the graph generation logic) is maintained. These unused events are periodically analyzed to identify potentially informative system behaviors, and the event processing code is iteratively updated to incorporate any event types that could improve graph completeness. As a result, all events relevant to system provenance are either included in node/edge creation, attribute enrichment, or are justified as omitted.

7. **Event-driven graph generation:** Each event may (i) create new nodes (e.g., new process, file, or job), (ii) connect existing nodes via a directed, annotated edge (e.g., process creates a file, process connects to an IP), or (iii) update attributes of an existing node or edge (e.g., increment crash count, update permissions, annotate file as executable). Event semantics are mapped precisely to graph operations, ensuring a comprehensive and information-rich provenance representation.

3.2.1.2 Event Source and ID Breakdown.

The following is the log sources and event IDs that are parsed and used for graph generation:

- **Sysmon:**
  - 1: *Process Creation*: Instantiates a process node (with process GUID, PID, image, command line) and links it to its parent process. All file paths referenced in the command-line are also extracted and linked via file_reference edges.
  - 2: *Creation Time Changed*: Adds edge (`file_creation_time_changed`) from process to file, with time attributes.

- 3: *Network Connection*: Adds edge (connects_to or connects_from) between process and IP address node, with protocol and port.
- 5: *Process Termination*: Updates process node termination time.
- 6: *Driver Loaded*: Adds (driver_loaded) edge from process to driver node.
- 7: *Image Loaded*: Adds (dll_loaded) edge from process to DLL node.
- 9: *RawAccessRead*: Adds (raw_access_read) edge from process to device node.
- 10: *ProcessAccess*: Adds (process_access) edge between two process nodes.
- 11: *FileCreate*: Adds (file_create) edge from process to file node.
- 12: *RegistryEvent (Create/Delete)*: Depending on the subtype, adds (registry_createkey, registry_deletekey, registry_deletevalue) edge from process to registry node.
- 13: *RegistryEvent (Value Set)*: Adds (registry_value_set) edge from process to registry node.
- 15: *FileCreateStreamHash*: Adds (file_stream_create) edge from process to file node.
- 17: *Pipe Created*: Adds (pipe_create) edge from process to pipe node.
- 18: *Pipe Connected*: Adds (pipe_connect) edge from process to pipe node.
- 22: *DNS Query*: Adds (dns_query) edge from process to domain node; domain resolves to IP via (resolves_to) edge.
- 24: *ClipboardChange*: Annotates process node with clipboard change count.
- 26: *File Delete Detected*: Adds (file_delete) edge from process to file node.
- 29: *Executable Detected*: Marks file node as executable.

• **Security:**
  - 4663: *File Access*: Adds (file_access) edge from process (resolved via Sysmon matching) to file node, with access mask.
  - 4670: *Permission Change*: Adds (change_permission) edge from process to file node, annotated with security descriptor changes.

• **Application:**
  - 1000: *Application Crash*: Increments crash count on process node (resolved via Sysmon matching).

• **BITS:**
  - 3: *BITS Service Created A New Job*: Adds (create_bits_job) edge from process to bits_job node.
  - 16403: *TBD*: Annotates bits_job node with transfer details.
  - 4: *Job Completion*: Adds (bits_job_file_transfer) edge from bits_job to file node.

- 5: *Job Cancelled*: Removes bits_job node.

- **TaskScheduler:**
  - 106: *Task Registered*: Adds scheduled_task node.
  - 200: *Action Started*: Adds (`create_task_instance`) edge from scheduled_task to scheduled_task_instance; links to process via (`task_instance_process`) edge.
  - 119, 107, 108, 118, 110: *Trigger Events*: Annotate scheduled_task_instance node with trigger type.

3.2.1.3 Node Types, Identifiers, and Attributes.

Table 2 summarizes all node types present in the provenance graph, including their typical identifiers and all attributes (annotations) that may be attached to each node during parsing and subsequent event processing.

Table 2: Node types, identifiers, and attributes in the provenance graph

Node Type	**Description**	**Node ID Format**	**Attributes**
process	Operating system process	`pro_`$ProcessGuid	`type`, `pid`, `process_guid`, `image`, `command_line`, `parent_guid`, `creation_time`, `termination_time`, `crash_count`, `clipboard_changes`
file	File or executable object	file path string	`type`, `is_executable`, `hash` (from ADS)
dll	Dynamic-link library	DLL file path string	`type`
driver	Kernel driver	driver filename	`type`
device	Device object	device name string	`type`
registry	Registry key or value	registry key path	`type`
pipe	Named pipe	`pipe::`$Name::$Timestamp	`type`, `name`, `created_at`
ip	IP address	IP string	`type`, `version`
domain	DNS domain	domain string	`type`
bits_job	BITS job object	job ID string	`type`, `job_id`, `user`, `job_title`, `remote_name`, `local_name`
scheduled task	Scheduled task	task name string	`type`, `user`
scheduled task instance	Task execution instance	instance ID string	`type`, `user`, `trigger`

3.2.1.4 Edge Types and Attributes.

Shared edge attributes: Most edges in the provenance graph are annotated with:

- `type`: Edge type as listed in the table.
- `timestamp`: UTC timestamp of the event.

- `occurrence`: Number of repeated occurrences of this edge (incremented if event is repeated).

Additional attributes are event-specific and listed in the table below.

Table 3: Edge types, source and destination nodes, and attributes

Edge Type	Source Node	Destination Node	Additional Attributes
process creation	process	process	–
process access	process	process	`granted_access`
process image	process	file / dll	–
file access	process	file	`access_mask`
file create	process	file	–
file reference	process	file	–
file creation time changed	process	file	`creation_time`, `previous_creation_time`
file stream create	process	file	`hash`
file delete	process	file	–
driver loaded	process	driver	–
dll loaded	process	dll	–
raw access read	process	device	–
registry createkey	process	registry	`event_type`
registry deletekey	process	registry	`event_type`
registry deletevalue	process	registry	`event_type`
registry value set	process	registry	`event_type`, `details`
pipe create	process	pipe	–
pipe connect	process	pipe	–
dns query	process	domain	–
create bits job	process	bits job	–
connects to	process	ip	`protocol`, `src_port`, `dest_port`
connects from	ip	process	`protocol`, `src_port`, `dest_port`
resolves to	domain	ip	–
bits job file transfer	bits job	file	`remote_name`
change permission	process	file	`original_sd`, `new_sd`
create task instance	scheduled task	scheduled task instance	–
task instance process	scheduled task instance	process	–

3.2.1.5 Implementation Details.

Several implementation strategies were adopted to maximize consistency, accuracy, and information richness in the graph:

- **Filename normalization:** All file and directory names in short 8.3 format (e.g., `ADMINI~1`) are converted to their full canonical form (`Administrator`) to ensure node uniqueness across different log sources.

- **Edge deduplication:** When an edge with the same source, destination, type, and unique attributes already exists, its `occurrence` attribute is incremented rather than duplicating the edge, thereby capturing frequency while preserving compactness.

- **Command-line enrichment:** each process creation event's command-line string is parsed to extract referenced file paths, and `file_reference` edges are created from the process node to these files. This enriches the provenance graph by capturing implicit dependencies and file usage relationships that might not be reflected in standard file access events.

- **Image path correction:** We observe that, in some cases, the image path associated with a process in Sysmon logs does not match the true image for a given GUID. To address this, the process creation event is always used to create or update the image path of a process node. This strategy ensures that the graph reflects the correct executable for each process. Such discrepancies are rare but can be critical for accurate attack reconstruction.

- **Event timing:** The careful selection of timestamps is crucial: Sysmon's timestamp is used for process creation (as it is typically more accurate and slightly earlier), while the system timestamp is used for process termination (as it is often later). This approach ensures that the calculated process lifetimes comprehensively encompass all events related to a process, regardless of which log source generated the event. This detail is especially important for correctly matching process activities across heterogeneous logs, particularly for short-lived or reused process IDs.

3.2.2 Node Labeling

Labeling the dataset is a laborious and time-consuming task, especially in our case, where each provenance graph contains tens of thousands of nodes and edges representing a vast mixture of benign and attacker-driven activity. Precise, granular labeling is critical for capturing the nuanced behaviors of APTs, whose malicious activity is often obscured among large volumes of regular system events. To address this challenge, we constructed per-attack, per-machine lists of Indicators of Compromise (IOCs), which are provided in structured YAML IOC files for each victim machine and attack day. These files list all first-level exploited processes, malicious files, attacker-controlled IP addresses and domain names, and scheduled tasks set up by the attacker. Such IOCs reliably capture the primary actions and entry points of the adversary, but do not account for all downstream effects of their behavior. For instance, if an attacker establishes a reverse shell on a victim system, the IOC file is guaranteed to include the reverse shell's process GUID. Still, not necessarily the numerous subprocesses spawned from that shell.

To ensure comprehensive and efficient annotation, we employ a set of label propagation rules that recursively extend malicious labeling from the IOC-identified nodes to related entities according to defined criteria. Starting from the high-confidence nodes in each IOC file, we automatically propagate the malicious tag to neighboring nodes that match behavioral or structural patterns characteristic of attacker activity. This propagation approach significantly reduces manual labeling effort, mitigates the risk of human error, and enables the detection of malicious behaviors that might arise from unknown or variant attack tools and techniques used in the simulations.

However, not every node related to attacker activity should necessarily be labeled as malicious. Some attacker behaviors, while clearly part of the intrusion process, are not inherently malicious when considered in isolation. For example, an attacker might install Python on a compromised system to support post-exploitation tooling. This installation creates numerous new files and processes, but labeling all of them as malicious would result in a large number of false positives in subsequent detection. To address this, we define a YAML-based whitelist in conjunction with the IOC file. The whitelist is used to prevent propagation rules from labeling specific files, processes, or other nodes as malicious, even if they are closely associated with attacker activity. This targeted whitelisting is essential for limiting over-labeling and ensuring that benign nodes, especially those associated with commonly used tools, are not incorrectly flagged as Malicious by the detection model.

3.2.2.1 Indicator-Driven Node Labeling.

We define a comprehensive set of IOCs, curated per attack campaign and stored as a YAML configuration file for each experiment. These IOCs span multiple entity types, including process GUIDs, process names, file paths, IP addresses, domain names, registry keys, scheduled tasks, and command-line substrings. Both inclusion (malicious) and exclusion (whitelist) lists are supported for each type, enabling precise discrimination even in environments with reused filenames or benign dual-use tools.
The labeling proceeds as follows:

- **Process GUID labeling:** Any process node whose globally unique process GUID matches a malicious GUID in the indicator set is marked as malicious.
- **Process name labeling:** Process nodes are labeled if their full image path or basename matches any entry in the process name indicator set.
- **File path labeling:** File and DLL nodes are labeled as malicious if their absolute path, basename, or parent directory (with wildcards supported) matches an indicator.
- **Network labeling:** IP and domain nodes are matched against the respective indicator sets.
- **Registry and task labeling:** Registry key and scheduled task nodes are checked for direct matches.
- **Command-line labeling:** Process nodes are labeled if their command-line begins with or contains an indicator substring.

A configurable whitelist for each entity type prevents over-labeling of nodes that may match common or benign indicators (e.g., PIDs reused across experiments).

3.2.2.2 Label Propagation.

Given the stealthy and multi-stage nature of APT attacks, direct indicator matching alone is insufficient to label all malicious activity. To overcome this, we employ iterative label propagation rules that reflect attacker

TTPs and graph semantics. During propagation, a configurable whitelist is also enforced to prevent uncontrolled "label explosion," ensuring that benign resources are not falsely classified. For example, if an attacker installs Ruby on a compromised host, the installation files and legitimate subprocesses are whitelisted and will not be flagged as malicious, despite being spawned by a malicious parent.

The propagation process includes:

- **Process-to-process propagation:** If a process node is labeled as malicious, all child processes (via process creation edges) are also labeled, unless whitelisted. Conversely, if a file or DLL node is labeled as malicious, all processes that load or execute that file (via process_image edges) are recursively labeled.
- **Pipe propagation:** Malicious processes that create named pipes mark those pipes as malicious, and any process interacting with a malicious pipe (via creation or connection) is recursively labeled, subject to whitelist checks.
- **Network and domain propagation:** Malicious domains propagate to their resolved IP nodes and vice versa, capturing infrastructure relationships.
- **Registry and resource propagation:** Malicious processes that create or modify registry keys, files, or scheduled tasks propagate their label to these resources.
- **Scheduled task propagation:** Labeled scheduled task nodes propagate to all task instances and processes they launch, and if a process is labeled, this label propagates back to the associated scheduled task instance.

Propagation is performed iteratively until convergence, ensuring transitive and context-aware labeling throughout the graph while the whitelist prevents benign dual-use tools and system resources from being overlabeled.

3.2.2.3 Final Label Assignment and Statistics.

After all direct and propagated labeling is complete, a boolean `malicious` attribute is assigned to every node in the graph. The final label distribution, both overall and per node type, is recorded for use in both evaluation and as metadata in the labeled graph files. Nodes not matched by any indicator or propagation rule are labeled as benign. This approach yields high-fidelity, fine-grained malicious node labeling, facilitating robust detection model development.

3.2.3 Feature Extraction

For effective learning on provenance graphs, each node must be represented by a comprehensive and semantically rich feature vector that captures both its structural role and its behavioral attributes. The challenge is to design features that are expressive enough to characterize the diverse node types and their relations, yet structured and consistent for downstream machine learning and graph neural network (GNN) models.

3.2.3.1 Feature Extraction Workflow.

Feature extraction is performed as a dedicated post-processing step on each labeled provenance graph. For every node, a high-dimensional feature vector is computed and exported, organized by node type. The workflow proceeds as follows:

1. **Schema-guided structural feature extraction:** For each node type, we determined which incoming and outgoing edge types are meaningful for that node. For each relevant edge type, we count both (i) the number of distinct edges of that type connected to the node (e.g., number of distinct files created by a process, number of unique IPs contacted by a process) and (ii) the total number of occurrences of that edge type by summing their `occurrence` attributes. This dual representation preserves both the diversity and the frequency of a node's interactions.

2. **Node-type-specific semantic features:**

    - *Files:* Path depth, executable/ script/ document flag, system directory location, suspicious extension, presence in temporary directories, file age, and access duration.
    - *Processes:* Hierarchical features (number of ancestors/ descendants/ children, maximum tree depth), image type (executable/ script/ system/ suspicious), system directory flag, lifetime in seconds, file-to-process creation time difference, command-line length, etc.
    - *Registry keys:* Registry hive, key depth, value length, complexity, path length, system/ startup/ persistence/ security key flags, suspicious location/key names, temporal access duration, and type indicators (binary/ string/ root/ deep key).

3. **Maliciousness label:** The ground truth "malicious" label (from the labeling phase) is appended to every node's feature vector for supervised learning.

4. **Type-specific export:** Extracted features for each node type are written as type-specific CSV files to support efficient model training and analysis.

3.2.3.2 Feature Set Structure.

Feature sets are centrally defined and extensible per node type. Each node type has:

- **Categorical features** (e.g., registry hive, file extension category)
- **Boolean indicators** (e.g., is_executable, is_system_file, is_suspicious_process)
- **Numerical features** (e.g., lifetime in seconds, key depth, file age)

Only features meaningful for each node type and observed relationships are computed, ensuring efficiency and minimizing noise.

3.2.3.3 Implementation Notes.

The extraction pipeline is fully automated and parallelized for scalability. Node features are computed using both intrinsic node attributes and graph-structural context (neighbor types, edge-type counts, and total interaction frequencies). Node-type-specific logic, for example, parsing process ancestry, classifying file extensions, and analyzing registry key structure, enables highly granular behavioral encoding. This design ensures the extracted features are directly usable for both interpretable analysis and high-performance learning models for malicious node detection and APT attribution.

3.2.4 Node Feature Autoencoder

Graphs collected from provenance data are inherently heterogeneous: different node types (such as `process`, `file`, `IP address`, or `registry_key`) come with distinct feature sets that vary widely in both dimensionality and semantics. Directly feeding these raw attributes into a downstream graph neural network is infeasible because the model expects a consistent fixed-length vector representation across all nodes. The role of the node feature autoencoder is therefore to unify these heterogeneous inputs into a shared embedding space that preserves type-specific information while aligning all nodes into a standard format suitable for graph learning. The remainder of this section outlines the training objective, the architecture of the autoencoder, the mechanics of its forward pass, the sampling strategy, and the key implementation details.

3.2.4.1 Training Objective.

Autoencoders are unsupervised neural architectures designed to learn compact representations by encoding input data into a latent vector and then reconstructing the original input from that representation. The training objective is to minimize the reconstruction error, which ensures that the learned embeddings retain sufficient information about the input features. In the context of provenance graphs, this principle is adapted to the heterogeneous setting: each node type has different feature sets, yet all must be projected into a unified latent space that preserves their semantic meaning while enabling comparability across types. Because each node type has its own decoder, the latent representations are optimized in such a way that they remain informative about the specific characteristics of their original type, while also being aligned in a common embedding space.

The reconstruction loss is formulated as the mean squared error (MSE) between the original and reconstructed features. MSE is particularly suitable in this setting for several reasons. First, all node features undergo preprocessing and normalization, which ensures that they are on comparable scales and bounded ranges, conditions under which MSE provides well-calibrated and interpretable error signals. Second, MSE yields smooth and stable gradients that are well suited for large-scale training with very large batch sizes. Finally, MSE directly penalizes deviations in proportion to their magnitude, aligning with the objective of maintaining high-fidelity reconstructions of diverse feature sets. These properties make MSE a principled choice for the heterogeneous node feature autoencoder.

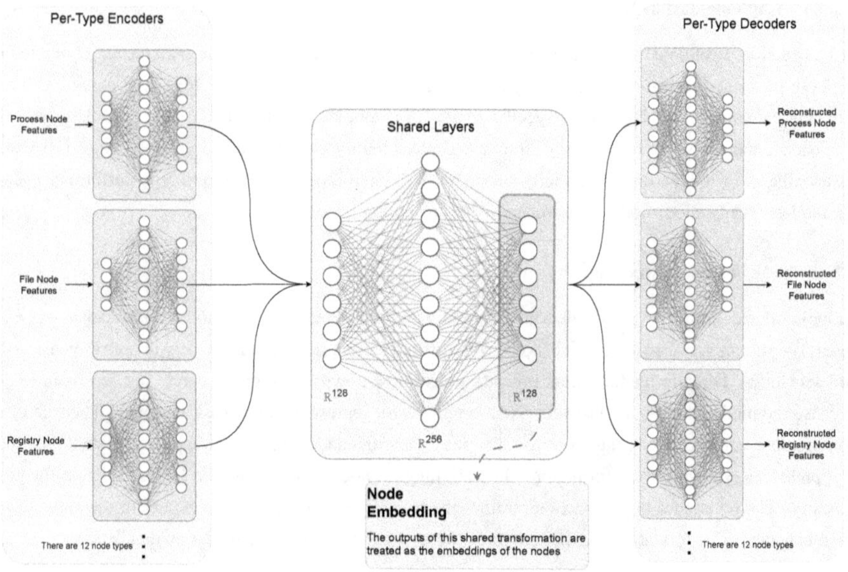

Figure 32: Schematic architecture of the heterogeneous node feature autoencoder. Each node type has its own encoder and decoder, while a shared fully connected alignment layer maps all embeddings into a common 128-dimensional space.

3.2.4.2 Architecture.

The autoencoder follows a type-specific design, where each node type has a dedicated encoder and decoder implemented as multilayer perceptrons. For a given node type with input dimensionality d, its encoder begins with a linear projection to a hidden dimension of 256, followed by a ReLU activation. Then it applies a second linear projection into a 128-dimensional embedding space. We tested several architectural configurations with deeper stacks, but the two-layer configuration consistently provided the best trade-off between stability and reconstruction accuracy. The embedding size was deliberately set to 128, slightly larger than the dimensionality of the process node feature space, which is the largest among all types, to avoid excessive compression and information loss. The high-level flow of this design is illustrated in Figure 32.

The embeddings produced by each type-specific encoder are then passed through a shared fully connected alignment layer, consisting of a Linear–ReLU–Linear stack ($128 \rightarrow 256 \rightarrow 128$). This layer enforces that representations from different node types are mapped into a common latent space while still retaining type-specific semantics. The outputs of this shared transformation are treated as the embeddings of the nodes and are used both for reconstruction and as downstream features.

Each node type also has a decoder that mirrors its encoder: a linear layer expands the embedding back to 256 hidden units, followed by a ReLU activation, and a reconstruction layer projects to the original feature dimensionality of that type. Weights of all linear layers are initialized using Xavier uniform initialization, and biases are set to zero, which stabilizes training at the beginning and ensures well-scaled gradients.

3.2.4.3 Forward Pass.

During the forward pass, a mini-batch is first padded to the maximum feature dimensionality across all types. Nodes are grouped by type, and their padded features are truncated to the actual feature width. A dropout of 5% is applied to the input features during training to reduce overfitting. Each type slice is then encoded by its dedicated encoder, aligned through the shared layer, and decoded back into the original feature space. The output of the shared alignment layer is considered the final embedding of each node and is returned for downstream tasks.

3.2.4.4 Sampling Strategy.

Training batches are generated using a stratified epoch sampling approach. At each epoch, a subset of training nodes is sampled with the following constraints: a maximum of 1.5 million samples per epoch, a minimum quota to ensure representation of rare types, and a maximum cap for overly frequent types. Rare categories can be oversampled with replacement when necessary. The resulting per-epoch batches therefore contain a balanced mixture of node types, preventing dominant types such as `process` or `file` from overwhelming the training signal and ensuring stable embeddings across the heterogeneous space.

3.2.4.5 Implementation Details.

Training proceeds for 80 epochs with a batch size of 2^{17} nodes. The optimizer is Adam with an initial learning rate of 5×10^{-4} and weight decay 10^{-5}. A linear warmup is applied during the first few epochs to stabilize convergence. Learning rate scheduling is handled by a reduction-on-plateau strategy, which decreases the learning rate by a factor of 0.5 if no improvement is observed for three consecutive epochs, down to a minimum of 10^{-7}. Mixed-precision training with bfloat16 is enabled on CUDA devices, significantly accelerating training while preserving numerical stability. To prevent gradient explosions, gradients are clipped to a maximum norm of 100. Validation is performed after each epoch on a hold-out split, with per-type reconstruction losses logged in detail. Specifically, the dataset is divided as follows: all but the last repetition of each attack scenario, together with all benign graphs, are used for training; from this training portion, 10% of nodes are randomly selected for validation in a stratified manner that guarantees at least ten samples per node type; and the last repetition of each attack scenario is withheld entirely as the test set. The best-performing model is tracked throughout training and restored when beneficial learning rate reductions occur.

Overall, by combining type-specific encoders and decoders, a shared alignment layer, stratified sampling, and carefully tuned training controls, the autoencoder produces 128-dimensional embeddings that are well-regularized, semantically meaningful, and balanced across node types. These embeddings provide the foundation for reliable downstream training of graph neural networks in the malicious node detection pipeline.

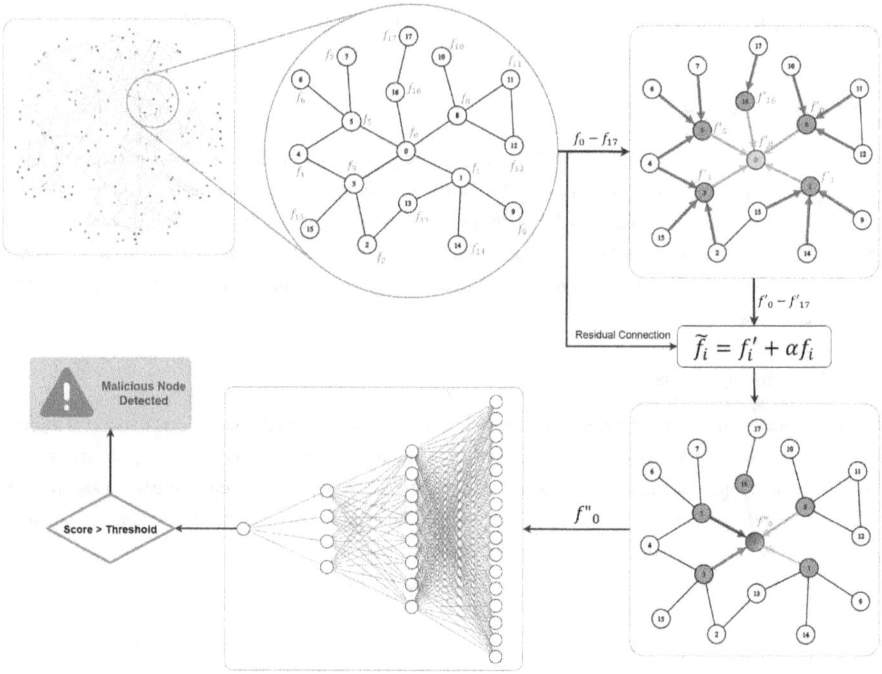

Figure 33: Architecture of the malicious node detection model. Node embeddings from the autoencoder are processed by a GraphSAGE layer with neighborhood sampling, followed by an edge-aware GAT layer that integrates edge types into the attention mechanism. A final feed-forward classifier maps the refined embeddings into benign or malicious predictions.

3.2.5 Malicious Node Detection Model

Detecting malicious nodes within a heterogeneous provenance graph is a crucial step in identifying APT-related behaviors. Once each node is represented by a fixed-length embedding vector, the next task is to train a model that can differentiate malicious nodes from benign ones based on their structural position in the graph, the semantics of the edges, and the encoded node features. In this section, we describe a supervised Graph Neural Network (GNN) that combines a GraphSAGE layer with an edge-aware Graph Attention (GAT) layer. The GraphSAGE layer provides scalability through neighborhood sampling, while the GAT layer assigns importance weights to neighbors and edge types, enabling the model to focus on the most relevant relationships for detection.

3.2.5.1 Model Overview.

Figure 33 demonstrates the overall workflow of the malicious node detection model. The process begins with the neighborhood selection around each seed node. The first GraphSAGE layer then aggregates features

from the fixed-size, sampled neighborhood. GraphSAGE is particularly suited for large provenance graphs because it avoids full-graph message passing, supports inductive inference on unseen nodes, and retains local structural context by combining sampled neighbor information with the node's own embedding.
The embeddings aggregated by GraphSAGE layer is then passed into a Graph Attention (GAT) layer augmented with edge attributes. The GAT uses a single attention head in this final layer. The reason behind this choice is that multi-head attention is often employed in intermediate layers to stabilize training and enrich features through concatenation, but at the final layer, a single head preserves a well-defined embedding dimensionality (no head-wise concatenation or averaging) and yields stable logits for the classifier. Attention coefficients depend on both neighbor embeddings and one-hot encoded edge types, which captures interaction semantics (for example, process creation, file access, registry modification, and network communication) and allows the network to assign higher weights to critical relations.
To further stabilize training and counter over-smoothing caused by the SAGE layer, the GAT is augmented with a learnable weighted residual connection. After applying the layer transformation and non-linearities, the output of the first SAGE layer is combined with the original input embedding scaled by a trainable scalar parameter. Unlike fixed skip connections, this design enables the model to tune the contribution of the residual pathway per layer adaptively. In practice, this ensures that essential node-specific signals are preserved while still benefiting from neighborhood aggregation.
Finally, a feed-forward classifier maps the refined embeddings into logits for making decisions between benign and malicious cases. Its architecture is:

$$\text{Linear}(128 \to 64) \to \text{ReLU} \to \text{Linear}(64 \to 32) \to \text{ReLU} \to \text{Linear}(32 \to 1).$$

Importantly, classification is only performed on the seed nodes of each batch, not on sampled neighbors. Seed nodes are the only ones for which a complete two-hop neighborhood of fixed size $[30, 10]$ is extracted; sampled neighbors may not include their entire neighborhood and thus lack a consistent structural context for fair scoring. During inference, probabilities are obtained from the logits of seed nodes, and a threshold is applied to generate binary predictions. The attention mechanism is also used to highlight which neighbors and edge types were most influential in each decision.

3.2.5.2 Graph Representation and Node/Edge Types.

As mentioned in section 3.2.4, node features are transformed into 128-dimensional embeddings using the autoencoder model. Edge types are one-hot encoded and incorporated into the GAT attention mechanism to preserve the semantics of different interaction types during classification. This provides a multi-relational graph for the subsequent node classification task.

3.2.5.3 Class Imbalance.

The main objective of malicious node detection is to maximize recall on malicious nodes while minimizing false alarms. Because malicious nodes are rare, representing only about 0.3% of all nodes, they are given much higher importance during training. Instead of processing the full graph of more than 14 million nodes in each epoch, the sampling procedure is designed so that the approximately 25,000 malicious nodes are revisited multiple times; each malicious node is expected to be sampled about eight times per epoch, a setting empirically shown to achieve high recall without excessive redundancy.

Each mini-batch is constructed by drawing 4096 seed nodes at random from the entire pool of graphs. Batches are not restricted to a single graph. In our design, seed nodes and their neighborhoods are classified independently of one another, so graph-level contiguity is unnecessary. Allowing cross-graph seed selection ensures that even graphs containing only a few malicious nodes contribute effectively to learning. For each seed, a two-hop neighborhood is constructed by sampling up to 30 neighbors at the first hop and up to 10 at the second hop. To improve generalization and avoid repeatedly presenting identical neighborhoods, 30% of each seed node's neighbors are randomly filtered out before sampling. In addition, each batch is constructed to contain approximately 20% malicious nodes. Given the natural rate of approximately 0.3%, this rebalancing ensures a sufficient number of positive samples for stable optimization.

Training employs a weighted binary cross-entropy objective. With batches containing roughly 20% positives, setting the positive class weight to 4 provides a balanced contribution between positive and negative samples, encouraging the model to learn discriminative boundaries for rare malicious behaviors without being overwhelmed by the abundance of benign nodes.

Note on neighborhood construction. In the standard PyTorch `NeighborSampler`, seed nodes selected from the same graph and their neighborhoods are merged into a unified subgraph for each batch. If two seeds are adjacent (directly or via neighbors), the resulting batch includes the entire merged subgraph, producing neighborhoods with widely varying effective sizes. This can destabilize training, especially for attention weights, because the model sees inconsistent structures across batches. In contrast, our sampler constructs each seed's two-hop neighborhood independently prior to classification, ensuring a consistent structural context for seed-wise scoring.

3.2.5.4 Training Procedure.

The model is trained with the Adam optimizer, dropout is applied in hidden layers for regularization, and gradient clipping at a global norm of 50 is used to prevent unstable updates. Each epoch consists of 256 batches, with a mini-batch size of 4096 seed nodes and gradient accumulation over 16 steps to offset the memory cost of attention. Evaluation during training is performed on 20 sampled batches for consistent monitoring.

Early stopping is employed to stop training once performance stabilizes, which in practice occurs after around 50 epochs. Learning-rate adaptation follows a reduction-on-plateau schedule: when the monitored metric stops improving for three consecutive epochs, the learning rate is reduced by a factor of 0.5, down to a minimum of 10^{-7}. The class-weight schedule is coordinated with this trajectory. Training begins with a positive class weight of 6 (negative class weight = 1) so the model emphasizes recall of malicious nodes, even at the cost of higher false positives. After roughly ten epochs, the learning rate is reduced according to the scheduler, and by around epoch fifteen the positive-class weight is decreased to 4. At this stage the model already identifies nearly all positives, and reducing the weight prioritizes boundary refinement to suppress false alarms. This staged strategy substantially improves recall while maintaining precision.

Inference, the model outputs a probability score for each seed node; applying a threshold yields binary predictions. The edge-aware attention mechanism provides interpretability by identifying which neighbors and edge types most strongly influenced each decision.

3.2.6 APT Attribution Module

The final stage of the framework focuses on attributing detected malicious activity to specific APT groups. While malicious node detection identifies compromised entities at the node level, attribution requires reasoning about larger structural patterns that characterize an attack campaign. To achieve this, the module first extracts malicious subgraphs around detected seeds and then classifies these subgraphs at the graph level using a dedicated GNN model. The overall GNN architecture of this model adheres to the same design principles as the malicious node detector, utilizing a GraphSAGE layer followed by an edge-aware GAT layer with residual connections.

3.2.6.1 Malicious Subgraph Extraction.

For each provenance graph, the trained malicious node detector from the previous section is first applied to every node, labeling them as malicious or benign. The set of malicious nodes identified in this way provides the basis for attribution. However, isolated malicious nodes rarely provide sufficient context. To address this, the system selects candidate *bridge nodes* from the two-hop neighborhood of the malicious nodes. These bridge nodes capture connecting structures that link otherwise separate malicious neighborhoods. The final subgraph is then constructed as the full one-hop neighborhood of the union of the malicious and bridge nodes. This ensures that the subgraph captures both the compromised entities and the immediate context of their interactions. Node features, edge indices, and one-hot edge attributes (encoding heterogeneous edge types such as process creation, file access, or registry modification) are retained to provide a faithful and semantically rich representation for downstream modeling.

3.2.6.2 Model Architecture.

As illustrated in Figure 35, each malicious subgraph is processed by the attribution model through a layered GNN architecture that mirrors the malicious node detection stage. A GraphSAGE layer is first applied to aggregate local neighborhoods in a scalable manner, followed by a GAT layer that incorporates edge attributes into its attention mechanism. Residual connections with learnable weights are applied between the input embeddings and the aggregated features, allowing the model to preserve node-specific signals while emphasizing relational dependencies. The final GAT layer uses a single attention head, reflecting the theoretical property that in the last layer of an attention-based GNN, multi-head attention is unnecessary since embeddings are collapsed into the final representation space.

The resulting node embeddings are then combined into a single graph-level representation using attention-based pooling, which enables the model to focus on the most informative nodes within each subgraph. This pooled vector is passed through a multi-layer classifier with progressively shrinking dimensions ($128 \rightarrow 64 \rightarrow 32 \rightarrow 7$), with ReLU activations applied between layers. The final layer outputs class scores for the

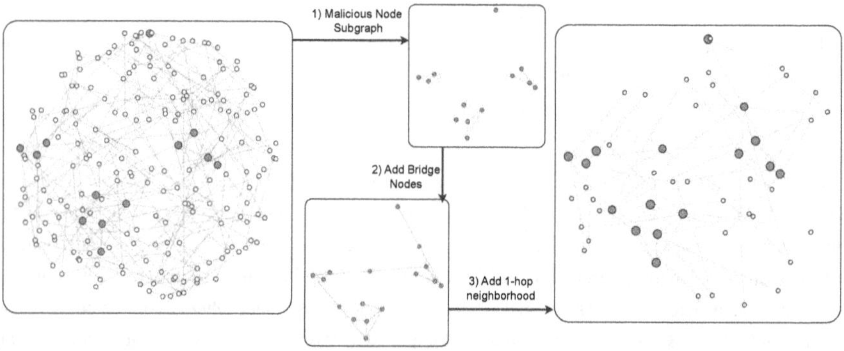

Figure 34: Illustration of the malicious subgraph extraction pipeline. Starting from the full provenance graph (left), (1) malicious nodes are first detected and isolated into a malicious-only subgraph, (2) bridge nodes are added from the two-hop neighborhood to connect disjoint malicious regions, and (3) the one-hop neighborhood of the malicious nodes is included to provide local context. The resulting subgraph (right) captures both compromised entities and their immediate interactions, preserving node features, edge indices, and heterogeneous edge types for downstream modeling.

predefined APT groups and the benign class, turning malicious subgraph patterns into a single graph-level prediction that represents the overall campaign.

3.2.6.3 Training Procedure.

The classifier is trained using cross-entropy loss, with class weights assigned inversely proportional to the frequency of each APT group. This adjustment addresses the natural imbalance in the dataset, where frequent groups, such as `MagicHound`, dominate over rare ones, like `FIN7` or `APT37`. Optimizer and learning rate scheduling follow the same setup as the malicious node detector, including Adam optimization, ReduceLROnPlateau scheduling, and gradient clipping to a maximum norm of 50. Training employs mini-batch processing at the subgraph level, with batches containing multiple subgraphs but ensuring that graph boundaries are respected.

To improve generalization, the attribution model applies up to 20% node dropout in the input subgraphs. As a result, in each epoch, each graph is sampled in five stochastic variations, ensuring that the model is exposed to slightly different realizations of the same campaign. This procedure is applied consistently during training and evaluation, so that performance metrics reflect robustness under dropout-induced variability. Given the dataset of 102 training graphs, this produces $102 \times 5 = 510$ subgraph instances per epoch.

To avoid noisy gradient updates from processing each graph individually, gradients are accumulated across 8 batches before performing an optimizer step. With 510 graphs per epoch, this strategy results in approximately $510/8 \approx 64$ effective parameter updates per epoch. Early stopping is applied once validation metrics converge, preventing overfitting while reducing computational cost.

By combining malicious subgraph extraction with a tailored GNN architecture that integrates GraphSAGE, edge-aware GAT, and residual connections, the attribution module elevates detection from the node level

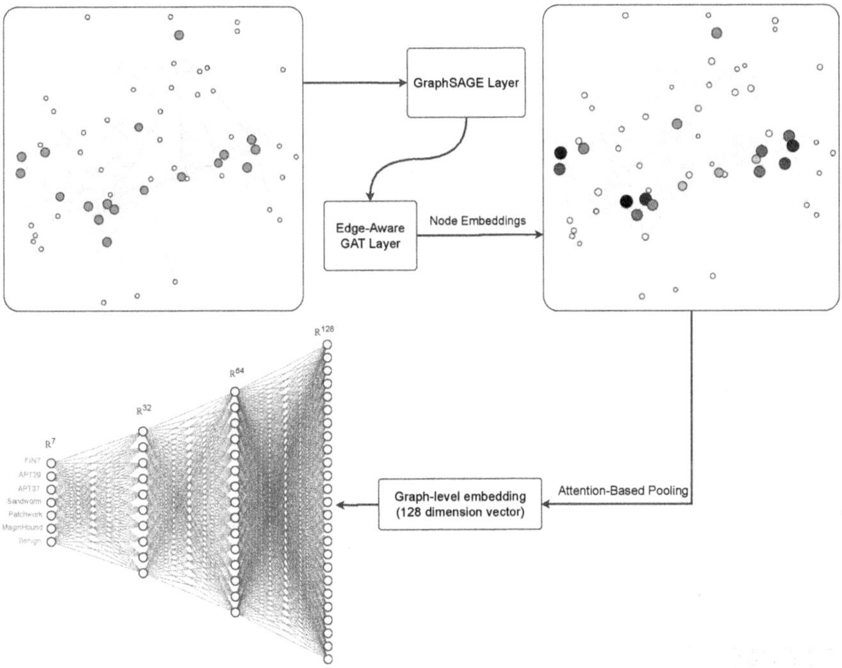

Figure 35: Architecture of the APT attribution module. Each malicious subgraph is encoded using a GraphSAGE layer followed by an edge-aware GAT layer with residual connections. Attention-based pooling aggregates node embeddings into a graph-level representation, which is then passed through a multi-layer classifier to predict the responsible APT group.

to the campaign level. Weighted training ensures fair learning across both frequent and rare APT groups, while global pooling and a structured classifier yield expressive graph-level representations. Together, these components enable fine-grained attribution of malicious activity to specific APT groups, providing actionable insights for advanced persistent threat analysis.

4 APT Dataset

This section introduces the dataset generated through the simulation of Advanced Persistent Threat (APT) attacks in a controlled laboratory environment, conducted from April 9th to May 14th, 2025. The primary objective of this work was to create a realistic and diverse collection of attack traces that would support the development and evaluation of advance persistent threat detection, classification, and profiling models.

4.1 Existing APT Datasets

A robust dataset is fundamental for evaluating APT detection methodologies. While several publicly available datasets exist, they exhibit significant limitations in attack diversity, operating system coverage, and the realism of attack scenarios. Table 4 provides a comparative overview of existing datasets based on key criteria, including the number of attack types (# AT), operating systems (OS), availability of raw data (RD), public accessibility (PA), standard behavior emulation (NBE), realism (RE), inclusion of known APT attacks (NAPT), duration of data capture (DC), and tools used for logging and data collection.

CICAPT-IIoT (2024) [58] captures a real-world APT29 attack scenario on a Linux environment using *Auditd* and *SPADE*. While it is a valuable dataset for provenance-based APT detection, it is limited in scope as it focuses solely on one APT attack over three days. Additionally, the dataset lacks raw system logs, which limits alternative analytical approaches beyond provenance-based detection.

Linux APT Dataset (2024) [59] provides a more diverse collection of APT attacks, covering four attack types and incorporating well-known APT groups, namely APT41, APT28, APT29, and Turla. This dataset is collected using *WAZUH*, an open-source security monitoring tool, and is notable for its long data collection period (October 2023 - January 2024). However, its exclusive focus on Linux environments limits its applicability to Windows-based infrastructures, which are common APT targets.

ATLAS (2020) [51] captures ten different APT scenarios within a Windows 7 (32-bit) environment. A key strength of ATLAS is its use of detailed logging tools such as *ETW (Sysmon, Firefox)* and *TShark*. However, each attack scenario lasts only an hour, which does not accurately reflect the stealthy nature of real-world APT attacks that often unfold over days or weeks. Additionally, the dataset does not include multi-host interactions, limiting its ability to simulate complex attack chains.

DARPA OpTC (2019) [60] provides a controlled APT experiment conducted on Windows 10 machines. The dataset captures attack sequences for one day per scenario using an *Apache Kafka* pipeline and is structured in the *eCAR* format. While it includes detailed logging mechanisms, it does not feature known APT groups and lacks raw data, restricting forensic analysis beyond the provided processed logs.

DARPA TC E3/E5 (2018-2019) [61] is one of the most comprehensive datasets in terms of attack diversity, containing 26 attack types executed across Windows 10, Linux, and FreeBSD platforms. Despite this diversity, the dataset does not include confirmed APT attack scenarios and primarily focuses on enterprise security use cases rather than APT-specific tactics.

MLAPT (2023) [62] focuses exclusively on network-based APT analysis, injecting attack traces into a baseline dataset. While it is valuable for network anomaly detection, it does not include real host-based attack traces and lacks public accessibility, restricting its usability for broader APT research.

Bon-APT (2023) [2] is one of the most extensive datasets in terms of attack samples, consisting of 120,000 Windows malware instances executed in a controlled Windows 10 (64-bit) environment using the *Cuckoo Sandbox*. However, it is primarily a malware execution dataset rather than a full APT scenario dataset, as it does not capture the multi-stage attack lifecycle characteristic of APT campaigns.
RT-APT (2024) [25] introduces provenance-based logging for APT analysis, collecting data on Ubuntu 16.04 systems using the *SPADE* provenance graph. Despite its strengths in tracking attack sequences, it does not include real-world APT group scenarios, and its attack data is limited to 24-hour engagements, which may not accurately represent the slower-paced APT operations.
Streamspot [63] dataset contains flow-graphs from system call traces of six scenarios, five benign (e.g., YouTube, Gmail, and gaming) and one attack. The attack is a drive-by download that exploits a Flash vulnerability to gain root access. While useful, the dataset has significant limitations: it's overly simplistic, lacks attack diversity, and relies on an outdated threat model (Flash exploits are no longer relevant). This limits its real-world applicability for modern attack detection.
APT-EXE [64] dataset provides valuable insights into APT execution behaviors but has key limitations. It only runs APT samples, rather than full attack scenarios, missing crucial stages such as reconnaissance, lateral movement, and data exfiltration. Execution issues arise as many samples fail due to missing dependencies or VM evasion. However, its benign data is well-collected and realistic, making it helpful in distinguishing between malicious and legitimate activity.

4.1.1 Limitations of the Existing Datasets

Despite their contributions to APT research, existing datasets exhibit several important shortcomings:

- **Short attack durations**: Many datasets only capture limited attack windows, often lasting just a few hours, whereas real APT campaigns unfold over weeks or months.
- **Outdated datasets**: Several widely used datasets are years old and no longer reflect the tactics, techniques, and procedures (TTPs) of modern threat actors.
- **Narrow scope of scenarios**: Some datasets are restricted to specific environments, such as Linux-only systems, and do not capture the diversity of operating systems, platforms, and attack surfaces found in real enterprises.
- **Lack of confirmed APT attacks**: Datasets such as DARPA TC E3/E5 rely on simulated techniques but do not represent real-world known APT groups observed in the wild.
- **Synthetic and simplified attack design**: Many datasets are generated from laboratory-controlled attacks on researcher-defined infrastructure. While useful for experimentation, these attacks often fail to reproduce the stealth, persistence, and multi-stage coordination of real APT campaigns.
- **Absence of multi-modal data**: The majority of datasets do not integrate host-based, network-based, and provenance-based data, nor do they provide other modalities such as binaries or memory traces, which limits the evaluation of advanced detection approaches.

Table 4: Comparison of Existing APT Datasets. **# AT**: Number of Attack Types. **OS**: Operating Systems Included. **RD**: Includes Raw Data. **PA**: Publicly Available. **NBE**: Normal Behavior Emulation. **RE**: Realistic Environment. **NAPT**: Includes Knwon APT attacks **DC**: Duration of Data Capture. **Tools**: Tools and format of the data captured.

Dataset	Year	# AT	OS	RD	PA	NBE	RE	NAPT	DC	Tools
CICAPT IIoT	2024	APT29	Linux	No	Yes	Yes 4 days	Yes	Yes	3 days, 45-75 mins interval	Auditd, SPADE
Linux APT Dataset	2024	4	Linux	Yes	Yes	Yes	Yes	Yes	Oct 2023 - Jan 2024	WAZUH
ATLAS	2020	10	Win7 (32-bit)	Yes	Yes	Yes	No single or 2 hosts	Yes	1 Hour per Attack	ETW (Sysmon, Firefox),TShark
DARPA OpTC	2019	3	Win10	No	Yes	Yes 4 days	Yes	No	1 day per attack	Apache Kafka, ETL server, eCAR format
DARPA TC E3/E5	2018 2019	26 (2 groups)	Win10, Linux, FreeBSD	No	Yes	Yes	Yes	No	9am-5pm	eCAR format
Bon-APT	2023	120,000 (Malware)	Win10 (64-bit)	Yes	No	Yes	No	No	N/A	Cuckoo Sandbox
RT-APT	2024	3	Ubuntu (16.04)	-	Yes	Yes	No	No	24h/attack	SPADE graph
APT-EXE	2020	4,790 Samples	Win 10	-	No	Yes	-	No	45 mins perattack	Procmon
StreamSpot	2016	single	Linux	No	Yes	Yes	No	No	-	Selenium RC

- **Data accessibility challenges**: Real-world enterprise telemetry is often proprietary, and operating systems are closed-source, making it difficult to obtain relevant and up-to-date data for research purposes.

To overcome these limitations, this research introduces a comprehensive and up-to-date dataset of simulated APT campaigns. The dataset captures diverse and recently observed attack scenarios, incorporates realistic adversarial tactics aligned with threat intelligence, and focuses on modern operating systems, particularly those based on Windows. It reflects realistic adversary behaviors, simulates long-term and stealthy attack progressions, and is designed to support reproducible evaluation for future APT detection research.

4.2 APT Groups Included in the Dataset

The dataset includes simulations of **FIN7**, **APT29**, **APT37**, and **Patchwork**, **Sandworm**, **Magic Hound**. These groups were selected due to their varied tactics and motivations, spanning cyber espionage, financial cybercrime, corporate intelligence gathering, ransomware operations, and Sabotage.
Table 7 provides a summary of the dataset, including the number of MITRE ATT&CK techniques employed by each APT group, a listing of those techniques, and a concise description of the attack behaviors captured. This dataset is designed as a comprehensive resource for researchers focused on modeling adversarial behavior, attack detection, and threat hunting within complex enterprise environments.

Motivation	APT Groups
Government and Military Espionage	APT1, APT28, **APT29**, APT5, APT19, APT33, **APT37**, APT41, APT-C-36, admin@338, Andariel, Aquatic Panda, Axiom, BackdoorDiplomacy, BlackTech, BRONZE BUTLER, Chimera, Dark Caracal, Darkhotel, Deep Panda, Elderwood, Ferocious Kitten, FIN13, Fox Kitten, Gamaredon Group, GALLIUM, Gallmaker, HEXANE, Higaisa, HAFNIUM, IndigoZebra, Inception, Ke3chang, Kimsuky, menuPass, Mofang, Molerats, MoustachedBouncer, MuddyWater, Mustang Panda, Naikon, Nomadic Octopus, OilRig, Poseidon Group, Rancor, Rocke, Scarlet Mimic, Scattered Spider, SideCopy, Sidewinder, Silence, Silent Librarian, SilverTerrier, Sowbug, Strider, TA2541, TA459, TA551, TeamTNT, The White Company, Tonto Team, Transparent Tribe, Turla, Volt Typhoon, Whitefly, Windigo, Windshift, WIRTE, ZIRCONIUM
Corporate and Industrial Espionage	APT3, APT10, APT12, APT18, APT30, LuminousMoth, Malteiro, Machete, **Patchwork**, PLATINUM, Winnti Group
Financial Cybercrime	APT38, Carbanak, Cobalt Group, DarkVishnya, EXOTIC LILY, FIN4, FIN5, FIN6, FIN8, FIN10, GCMAN, GOLD SOUTHFIELD, Indrik Spider, Lazarus Group, Metador, RTM, TA505, Wizard Spider
Ransomware Operations	**FIN7**, FIN8, Indrik Spider, Wizard Spider, TA505
Political and Ideological Goals	**Magic Hound**, Confucius, CopyKittens, CURIUM, Ember Bear, Gorgon Group, LAPSUS$, PLATINUM, POLONIUM, PROMETHIUM, Stealth Falcon
Disruption and Sabotage	Moses Staff, **Sandworm Team**
Cyber Warfare	Dragonfly

Table 5: APT Groups Categorized by Motivation (Implemented APTs are in **bold**)

Table 6: Number of techniques per tactic for top 50 APT groups based on MITRE ATT&CK framework. **Abbreviations:** IA=Initial Access, EX=Execution, PE=Persistence, PR=Privilege Escalation, DE=Defense Evasion, CA=Credential Access, DI=Discovery, LM=Lateral Movement, CO=Collection, C2=Command and Control, EXF=Exfiltration, IM=Impact, **Total**=Sum of all techniques.

Group	IA	EX	PE	PR	DE	CA	DI	LM	CO	C2	EXF	IM	**Total**
Lazarus Group	5	7	0	7	22	2	10	2	6	11	2	6	**80**
APT28	8	6	3	5	14	7	4	3	12	9	3	1	**75**
APT41	5	5	3	5	17	6	11	4	2	9	1	2	**70**
Kimsuky	5	7	4	6	16	5	8	3	7	6	2	0	**69**
APT32	4	10	2	5	20	4	10	5	1	5	2	0	**68**
Magic Hound	6	6	2	4	13	2	12	2	6	8	1	1	**63**
Wizard Spider	5	6	3	6	8	6	8	7	5	2	3	2	**61**
Turla	3	7	2	6	7	2	18	2	4	7	1	0	**59**
Chimera	3	5	1	1	6	4	18	5	8	4	2	0	**57**

Group	IA	EX	PE	PR	DE	CA	DI	LM	CO	C2	EXF	IM	**Total**
MuddyWater	3	11	1	2	11	6	9	1	3	8	1	0	**56**
OilRig	5	7	2	1	6	9	15	1	2	6	1	0	**55**
Sandworm Team	8	6	1	0	7	5	8	3	2	7	1	5	**53**
APT39	4	8	4	3	6	6	6	2	5	6	1	0	**51**
Threat Group-3390	7	5	1	5	10	5	7	2	5	2	2	0	**51**
APT29	8	6	4	6	9	6	1	1	2	7	0	0	**50**
FIN13	3	4	3	4	6	5	10	4	3	4	0	2	**48**
Dragonfly	6	6	2	3	7	6	8	2	5	2	0	0	**47**
Gamaredon Group	1	7	1	2	13	0	6	3	5	4	2	2	**46**
FIN7	7	9	1	3	7	1	3	3	3	6	1	1	**45**
menuPass	4	5	0	2	11	4	6	2	7	3	0	0	**44**
APT3	2	4	2	4	7	5	9	2	3	4	1	0	**43**
Ke3chang	3	3	0	2	4	6	12	1	6	3	2	0	**42**
APT38	2	6	1	2	9	2	8	0	2	2	0	7	**41**
Mustang Panda	3	7	1	2	9	1	6	0	4	5	1	0	**39**
FIN6	3	7	0	4	5	5	3	1	6	4	1	0	**39**
BRONZE BUTLER	2	6	0	3	10	1	6	2	4	5	0	0	**39**
Tropic Trooper	3	4	1	4	8	0	10	0	1	6	2	0	**39**
Patchwork	3	7	1	3	10	1	4	1	4	3	0	0	**37**
Fox Kitten	2	3	3	1	5	4	7	4	4	4	3	1	**37**
Leviathan	4	6	3	3	6	2	6	2	2	4	4	1	**37**
TeamTNT	1	3	1	3	9	2	8	2	7	3	5	2	**37**
FIN8	3	5	1	4	5	1	7	2	6	4	4	1	**34**
Volt Typhoon	2	3	1	0	4	3	14	1	4	4	2	0	**34**
Earth Lusca	3	6	1	2	8	2	7	1	7	2	3	1	**34**
Cobalt Group	3	7	0	6	7	1	6	2	2	6	2	1	**33**
TA505	3	8	1	2	8	2	6	2	3	3	3	0	**30**
GALLIUM	3	3	2	1	6	2	4	1	4	3	2	1	**29**
APT33	3	5	1	3	5	3	6	1	4	2	3	2	**29**
APT37	2	7	0	2	8	1	5	1	3	2	3	2	**29**
Rocke	1	1	1	3	11	1	3	2	3	4	3	2	**29**
Sidewinder	2	6	1	1	7	1	8	1	4	2	2	0	**28**
Silence	2	5	1	1	7	1	5	1	3	2	3	1	**27**

Group	IA	EX	PE	PR	DE	CA	DI	LM	CO	C2	EXF	IM	**Total**
HEXANE	1	4	1	1	6	1	6	1	2	2	1	0	**26**
Higaisa	2	4	1	2	7	1	6	1	0	1	1	0	**26**
ToddyCat	3	3	1	1	6	2	3	1	4	2	1	0	**25**
HAFNIUM	3	2	1	2	5	1	6	1	3	1	1	0	**25**
APT5	2	4	2	2	5	1	6	1	0	1	1	0	**25**
Darkhotel	3	4	0	2	5	2	7	2	2	0	1	0	**24**
Scattered Spider	1	2	2	2	5	2	5	1	2	1	1	0	**24**
TA2541	2	5	1	2	5	1	3	1	3	1	1	0	**22**

4.3 Selection Criteria

The dataset aims to comprehensively cover APT groups across multiple categories, ensuring that a wide range of attack techniques and strategies are represented. The selected APT groups have been chosen based on their recent activity, diversity in attack methodologies, and relevance to current cyber threats. Six distinct APT groups, namely FIN7, APT29, APT37, Patchwork, Sandworm, and Magic Hound, were selected for simulation, each based on their documented real-world campaigns and unique attack methodologies. For every group, their characteristic Tactics, Techniques, and Procedures (TTPs) were faithfully replicated, ensuring the dataset closely reflects the multi-stage behavioral patterns observed in authentic incidents.
The selection of APT groups was based on the following criteria:

- **Recent Activity**: The dataset prioritizes APT groups that have been active in recent years to ensure relevance in detecting modern attack patterns.
- **Technique Diversity**: APTs using a considerable range of diverse techniques across the MITRE ATT&CK framework, such as credential dumping, lateral movement, and data exfiltration, were prioritized.
- **Targeted Platforms**: Given the prevalence of Windows-based environments in real-world attacks, APTs known for targeting Windows infrastructures were emphasized.
- **Multi-Stage Attacks**: Groups demonstrating complex, multi-stage attack chains were included to provide a comprehensive dataset for evaluating detection mechanisms.

By incorporating these APTs, the dataset ensures a robust foundation for evaluating security mechanisms against a broad spectrum of threats. The additional planned attack scenarios will further improve the dataset's coverage and effectiveness in training detection models.

4.4 Timeline

Each attack scenario was executed on a separate day (Monday through Saturday each week), following the attack lifecycle typical for the corresponding APT group. This scheduling not only introduces temporal separation and variety across the dataset but also, through repeated attacks by certain groups, enables modeling of realistic variation in attacker behavior. Each repetition contributed to the diversity of the dataset, incorporating changes such as the order of attacker actions, variation in command-and-control infrastructure, communication protocols, and minor adjustments to malware drop paths. Figures 36 and 37 illustrate the schedule of APT attack scenarios across April and May 2025, detailing the temporal distribution of each group's campaigns.

April **2025**

MONDAY	TUESDAY	WEDNESDAY	THURSDAY	FRIDAY	SATURDAY	SUNDAY
31	01	02	03	04	05	06
07	08	09 FIN7	10 APT29	11 APT37	12 Patchwork	13
14 Sandworm	15 Magic Hound	16 FIN7	17 APT37	18 Sandworm	19 Magic Hound	20
21 Patchwork	22 APT29	23 Sandworm	24 Patchwork	25 Magic Hound	26 FIN7	27
28 APT29	29 APT37	30 APT37	01	02	03	04

Figure 36: Dataset Generation Calendar (April 2025): Daily schedule of simulated APT attacks.

4.5 Infrastructure Overview

To effectively analyze Advanced Persistent Threat (APT) attack behavior, a controlled network infrastructure has been designed and implemented. This infrastructure simulates a realistic organizational environment with distinct network segments: **Internal Network, DMZ (Demilitarized Zone), and External Network**. The setup ensures controlled interaction between adversarial attack machines and organizational assets, allowing for precise monitoring and evaluation of attack tactics, techniques, and procedures (TTPs).
Figure 38 illustrates the setting of the testbed used for dataset collection and attack evaluation. The infrastructure consists of the following components:

- **Internal Network**: Contains critical enterprise services, including an **Active Directory (AD) domain**

Figure 37: Dataset Generation Calendar (May 2025): Daily schedule of simulated APT attacks.

controller, **DNS server**, **mail server (Microsoft Exchange)**, and several **Windows workstations** representing employee machines. This network is isolated from direct external access.

- **DMZ (Demilitarized Zone)**: Hosts a **public-facing web server**, which acts as an entry point for external interactions. This server is exposed to potential attacks from adversaries in the external network.
- **External Network**: Simulates the attack environment, where adversary-controlled machines, both Linux and Windows-based, attempt to exploit vulnerabilities in the DMZ and, potentially, pivot into the internal network.
- **ACL and Routing Table**: The Access Control List of the Switch, along with the *iptables* set on the router, which brings internet access to the network, enforces access control policies, restricting direct access between networks except for designated communication paths depicted in Figure 38 using arrows.

4.6 Data Collection

To systematically evaluate attacker behaviors, a comprehensive set of Windows event logs and network traffic data was collected during the simulation of APT campaigns.

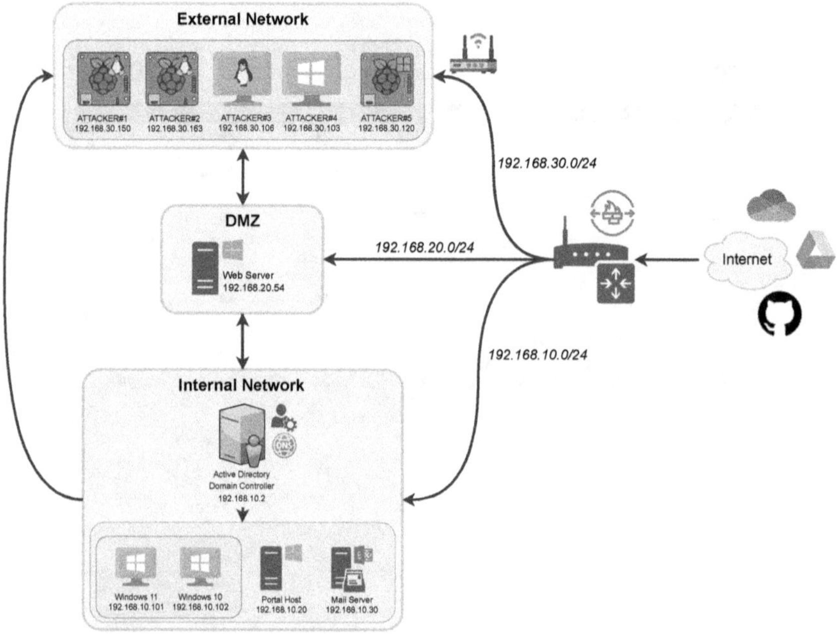

Figure 38: Network Infrastructure for APT Attack Simulation

4.6.1 Log Collection

A comprehensive set of Windows event logs was collected to capture a wide range of host activities:

- **Security Logs**: Record authentication attempts, account logon events, file access events, and privilege use, which are critical for tracking attacker access and escalation.
- **Application Logs**: Contain events generated by applications and services, often highlighting abnormal behavior or software misuse during attacks.
- **Sysmon Logs**: Provide fine-grained monitoring of system activity. The following Sysmon events were captured: *ProcessCreate, ProcessTerminate, FileCreateTime, FileCreate, FileExecutableDetected, FileCreateStreamHash, FileDeleteDetected, NetworkConnect, DnsQuery, DriverLoad, ImageLoad, CreateRemoteThread, RawAccessRead, ProcessAccess, PipeEvent, WmiEvent, RegistryEvent, ClipboardChange, and ProcessTampering*.
- **BITS Logs**: Capture events related to Background Intelligent Transfer Service, which adversaries may abuse for stealthy file transfers and persistence.

- **Task Scheduler Logs**: Track scheduled task creation, modification, and execution, a standard method for maintaining persistence.
- **System Logs**: Report operating system and driver events, including service startups and failures that may be linked to malicious activity.
- **Group Policy Logs**: Reflect the application of domain policies that can be targeted or modified by attackers to establish control or deploy malicious configurations.

All event logs were centrally collected using the domain controller. A Group Policy Object (GPO) named `ExportEventLogs` was configured to run every hour, staging the desired log files under `C:\Temp\EventLogExports`. These files were then copied to a remote storage drive (`192.168.1.3`) using `robocopy`. To ensure continuity, the target log files were set to archive when reaching their maximum size limit automatically.

4.6.2 Network Traffic Collection

Network data was captured in `pcap` format using the port mirroring (SPAN) capability of a Cisco switch. This enables deep packet inspection and provides supplementary visibility into network-layer APT techniques such as lateral movement and data exfiltration.

Log Collection Process: All event logs were centrally collected using the domain controller. A Group Policy Object (GPO) named `ExportEventLogs` was configured to run every hour, staging the desired log files under `C:\Temp\EventLogExports`. These files were then copied to a remote storage drive (`192.168.1.3`) using `robocopy`. To ensure continuity, the target log files were set to automatically archive when they reached their maximum size limit.

This structured collection process guarantees comprehensive coverage of both host and network activities, providing a robust foundation for analyzing APT behaviors.

4.7 Benign Behavior Simulation

To create realistic background activity and distinguish malicious events from normal usage, benign user behavior was simulated on all machines. This was achieved through a GPO named `SimulateBenignBehavior`, applied from the domain controller. The simulated actions differed based on machine role:

- **Servers:** Activities focused on administrative tasks such as creating and deleting notes, configuration files, and report files in various formats. Servers also executed monitoring tools (e.g., Task Manager) and ran PowerShell commands to inspect active processes.
- **Workstations:** Activities reflected developer employee behavior. These included watching online videos, browsing websites using Selenium, sending emails, building and running projects in Visual Studio (.NET) and Android Studio, and occasionally executing Git commands.

This structured setup ensures comprehensive visibility into both host and network activities, while also embedding realistic benign behaviors and reproducibility measures to reflect real-world enterprise environments better.

4.8 System Imaging and Restoration

To ensure reproducibility and consistency across all attack simulations, **Clonezilla** was used to capture baseline images of all victim machines after completing initial configurations. After each attack day, all systems were reimaged from these baseline snapshots, guaranteeing a clean and controlled environment for subsequent experiments.

4.9 Attack Scenarios

This section describes the APT groups and the representative campaigns implemented in our dataset. Each campaign is organized into discrete stages, and for every stage, we provide a straightforward, stage-specific narrative and a structured breakdown that includes exploited vulnerabilities, the malware samples employed (with SHA-256 hashes), and the corresponding MITRE ATT&CK technique identifiers.
Note: command-level logs, execution timestamps, and detailed operational notes are provided in the Appendix 6 section.

4.9.1 FIN7

FIN7, also known as Carbon Spider, is a financially motivated advanced persistent threat (APT) group that has been operating since at least 2013. Their campaigns have primarily focused on industries such as retail, hospitality, financial services, and utilities in the United States, consistently using sophisticated and evolving tactics to infiltrate targets and exfiltrate valuable information [65].

4.9.1.1 Initial Access

FIN7 has steadily expanded its arsenal for gaining initial access. While phishing was traditionally the primary method, recent years have seen the incorporation of software supply chain compromise and the exploitation of stolen credentials [66]. Since April 2022, the group has been observed exploiting a chain of Microsoft Exchange Server vulnerabilities (CVE-2021-31207, CVE-2021-34523, and CVE-2021-34473). This combination enables attackers to bypass authentication, impersonate arbitrary users, and execute arbitrary file writes, ultimately resulting in remote code execution (T1190). These exploits enable them to escalate from low-privileged credentials to SYSTEM-level access on Exchange Servers, granting the ability to execute any command remotely [67]. In practice, following initial access, the group swiftly removes mailbox exports and related draft emails to cover their tracks.

4.9.1.2 Execution

Once inside the environment, FIN7 relies on multiple PowerShell code families (T1059, T1059.001, T1564.003) for post-exploitation. Notably, the POWERTRASH loader[1], an in-memory dropper (T1620), is used to execute an embedded Cobalt Strike beacon [66]. Secondary access is established with the BEACON (T1571), after which the group performs enumeration (T1033) using both Windows-native tools and open-source

[1] SHA256: 662124b0c998fd0826c192514b1f57f8002f2ab031996aa6dd7832f561679779

modules, such as PowerSploit (T1588.002), as well as PowerShell-based Kerberoasting for credential access (T1558.003, T1069.002). The attackers then deploy an obfuscated loader (T1027) for a custom variant of the PowerShell-based POWERPLANT backdoor[2], usually version "0.028" as observed in the wild, to provide tertiary access (T1059.003). The POWERPLANT framework supports the dynamic delivery of additional modules from its command-and-control (C2) server, including EASYLOOK and BOATLAUNCH (T1105).

4.9.1.3 Reconnaissance

EASYLOOK, a reconnaissance module in active use by FIN7 since at least 2019, gathers extensive data from compromised systems: operating system version, registration keys, hostnames, user and domain data (T1087.002), and hardware information (T1082). The POWERPLANT C2 delivers the latest version of EASYLOOK in PowerShell form, and it conducts a check for virtualized or sandbox environments before data collection (T1497.001), helping to evade automated analysis.

4.9.1.4 Defense Evasion and Persistence

FIN7's persistence techniques involve repeated attempts to deploy POWERPLANT with obfuscation (T1027, T1059.003). For defense evasion, the group uses BOATLAUNCH[3] (T1218.011), a helper module sent by the POWERPLANT C2. BOATLAUNCH continually scans for unpatched PowerShell processes (T1057) and, for each, locates and patches `amsi.dll!AmsiScanBuffer` with a five-byte instruction to always return S_OK, thereby bypassing the Windows Antimalware Scan Interface (AMSI) [66]. PowerShell TLS certificate verification is also disabled, allowing unrestricted download and execution of additional payloads.

4.9.1.5 Historical Evolution and Ransomware Deployment

FIN7 initially targeted point-of-sale (POS) devices to steal payment card information, which was then monetized through illicit forums [68]. From April 2020 onward, their focus shifted to "big game hunting" operations, deploying REvil ransomware and later their own Ransomware-as-a-Service (RaaS), Darkside [65]. After Darkside ceased operations following the Colonial Pipeline attack in May 2021, FIN7 returned in July 2021 with BlackMatter, a RaaS strain aimed mainly at organizations in the US, Canada, Australia, and the UK, while avoiding the healthcare and government sectors [69]. Analysis shows that BlackMatter shares significant code similarities with Darkside, pointing to common authorship. The group has run these ransomware payloads under benign-looking names such as `sleep.exe` (T1036), encrypting files for impact (T1486) and collecting data from local systems (T1005).

4.9.1.6 BlackMatter Ransomware Technical Details

BlackMatter[4] uses a combination of RSA-1024 and a modified ChaCha20 cipher for file encryption (T1560, T1486), with the ChaCha20 matrix protected similarly to REvil [70]. Its entire configuration, including the

[2]SHA256: 4cdd13ce346a3407ea5109a72f0b59d6a2fad3255719cbaf16947b58fdfd7513
[3]SHA256: 454afe23c5e0c3d535e5f0794e838ca98fb23a55181a657aa1004df814ea1ddc
[4]SHA256: 22d7d67c3af10b1a37f277ebabe2d1eb4fd25afbd6437d4377400e148bcc08d6

RSA public key for file encryption (T1573.002), victim identifiers, AES key for encrypted C2 communications (T1071.001, T1132.001), C2 server URLs, lists of services to terminate, and other operational flags, is itself AES-encrypted and aPLib-compressed in process memory. When C2 URLs are specified, BlackMatter encrypts information about the victim system and encryption statistics with a hard-coded AES key before sending this data via TCP (T1095).

To accelerate file encryption, BlackMatter's threads use a shared structure for task division. The ransom note is also encrypted within the configuration, then dynamically decrypted and written as ".README.txt" into every directory (T1140). API calls in the ransomware are obfuscated using runtime resolution and hash-based string comparison (T1027.010), which complicates static analysis. During execution, BlackMatter verifies its privilege level by checking if it is running with administrative rights, querying system version, and validating the process token's membership in admin groups (T1069.002). If not running as an administrator, BlackMatter performs a UAC bypass by registering itself as "dllhost.exe" in the ProcessParameters of its PEB and relaunches itself with elevated privileges using the ShellExecute function of the ICMLuaUtil interface. It then terminates the non-elevated instance.

The ransomware generates a unique encrypted file extension for each victim using the system's machine GUID (T1012), with special character substitutions to ensure compatibility. The same extension is used as a prefix for ransom note filenames. Eleven different key buffers are randomly created for use depending on file size. When launched with the `-safe` flag and if the process token is in `DOMAIN_ALIAS_RID_ADMINS`, BlackMatter forces a reboot into safe mode to run with fewer defensive restrictions. Persistence is maintained by setting a randomly generated registry value in `SOFTWARE\Microsoft\Windows\CurrentVersion\RunOnce` (T1547.001). BlackMatter also attempts to duplicate tokens from elevated processes (T1055) and, before enabling safe boot, performs undocumented wallpaper operations, issuing a system reboot via NtShutdownSystem.

Before encryption, the ransomware wipes the Recycle Bin on all drives (T1070.004, T1083) and, if configured, terminates and deletes specified services by their hashed names. Data is sent to remote servers both before and after encryption (victim system details are exfiltrated before encryption (T1082), while encryption statistics are sent after encryption). All such communications are encrypted using AES and Encoded in Base64.

4.9.2 APT29

APT29, also known as Midnight Blizzard or Nobelium, is a state-sponsored advanced persistent threat (APT) group linked to Russian intelligence services. Active since at least 2008, APT29 has conducted sophisticated cyber-espionage operations targeting government and private-sector entities worldwide, and is responsible for notable campaigns such as the SolarWinds supply chain compromise, in which the SUNBURST backdoor was embedded into the Orion IT monitoring platform and deployed to numerous organizations globally [71, 72, 73].

4.9.2.1 Initial Access

APT29 employs a variety of initial access techniques, including spear-phishing emails, credential theft, and exploitation of on-premises environments [71]. Notably, the group has leveraged rogue RDP techniques, deploying PyRDP-based man-in-the-middle attacks to intercept authentication credentials and session tokens [74]. Since October 2024, Microsoft Threat Intelligence has observed APT29 targeting individuals in government, academia, defense, NGOs, and other sectors through spear-phishing emails containing Remote Desktop Protocol (RDP) configuration files, signed with LetsEncrypt certificates. These files, sent to thousands of targets across more than 100 organizations, established RDP sessions with actor-controlled servers when opened [75]. This process may expose the credentials of the signed-in user and allow the attacker to interact with a wide range of target system resources, including:

- Files and directories
- Connected network drives
- Connected peripherals, including smart cards, printers, and microphones
- Web authentication using Windows Hello, passkeys, or security keys
- Clipboard data
- Point of Service (POS) devices

This level of access enables the adversary to deploy malware or remote access trojans (RATs) on local drives and mapped network shares, especially in AutoStart folders, or to install additional tools to maintain persistence after the RDP session closes (T1566.001, T1204.002, T1078, T1133, T1589, T1021.001, T1105). In observed campaigns, an employee with access to a public-facing web server outside the organization's main network receives an RDP file via phishing email (T1566.001). When the attachment is executed (T1204.002), the RDP session is established to a PyRDP server controlled by the attacker, capturing authentication credentials and clipboard content [74]. Using these stolen credentials (T1078, T1133, T1589), the attacker connects to the web server and then pivots to establish RDP connections to internal Windows servers within the corporate environment [76] (T1078.002, T1078.003). To minimize network traces, a Caldera agent is deployed on internal servers, facilitating further covert activity (T1105).

4.9.2.2 Establishing Presence and C2

After initial access, and except during the first week of our simulation, Caldera agents were deployed on both the mail server and domain controller (DC). Domain-related enumeration and administrative actions (such as querying Active Directory and group memberships) were executed on the DC. At the same time, email exports and exfiltration operations took place on the mail server. Actions including firewall rule modification, Chrome cookie theft, and deployment of persistence mechanisms (such as the Sibot scheduled task) were orchestrated from both Caldera agents to maximize coverage [71, 76] (T1105, T1562).

Internal Reconnaissance and Lateral Movement:

Once inside, APT29 leveraged PowerShell for advanced enumeration of Exchange and Active Directory. The attacker used commands such as `Get-ManagementRoleAssignment`, `Get-ADUser`, and `Get-ADGroupMember` on the DC to enumerate users and groups (T1087.002), and `Get-WebServicesVirtualDirectory` to retrieve Exchange server configuration (T1083) [73]. The attacker also employed the utility `sqlceip.exe`, a disguised version of AdFind from joeware.net (T1059.003, T1036.005), for extensive Active Directory reconnaissance.

The attacker used AdFind for a range of Active Directory discovery operations [73]:

- **Enumerate Active Directory Admins:** Listing users and groups with administrative privileges (T1087.00
- **Enumerate Active Directory Exchange AD Objects:** Extracting information on Exchange-related AD objects.
- **Account Discovery: Domain Account:** Enumerating domain user accounts for lateral movement (T1087.002).
- **Enumerate Active Directory Domain Controller Objects:** Mapping core authentication infrastructure.
- **Enumerate Active Directory Subnet Objects:** Discovering AD subnet objects to learn about segmentation and topology.
- **Enumerate Active Directory OUs:** Listing Organizational Units to understand logical domain structure.
- **Enumerate Active Directory Trusts:** Identifying domain and forest trusts for potential cross-domain access.
- **Enumerate Active Directory User Objects:** Gathering user object details to support privilege escalation.
- **Listing Password Policy:** Extracting password policy settings to inform password attacks.

Stolen credentials allowed the attacker to move laterally and access further systems via RDP and SMB (T1078.002, T1078.003, T1558, T1555). The group was also observed modifying system firewall rules to enable persistent remote SMB and RDP access [76] (T1562).

4.9.2.3 Persistence and Defense Evasion

For persistence, APT29 scheduled tasks that mimicked legitimate system processes. Due to the unavailability of the SUNSPOT implant, the simulation deployed Sibot, a PowerShell-based malware described in Microsoft's analysis [77]. Sibot was scheduled on both servers for redundancy and stealth. The Sibot loader[5]

[5]SHA256: e9ddf486e5aeac02fc279659b72a1bec97103f413e089d8fabc30175f4cdbf15

and its second-stage payload[6] maintained callback to C2 infrastructure (T1059.001, T1053.005, T1587.001). Scheduled task names were chosen to resemble legitimate Windows processes (e.g., "\Microsoft\Windows\CertificateServicesClient\AikCetnrll") to evade detection (T1036.004). Defense evasion techniques included deleting exported mailbox data and modifying logs (T1070.008, T1070.004, T1562), as well as using Caldera agents for covert command and control [71, 76].

4.9.2.4 Data Collection and Exfiltration

On the mail server, email data from targeted accounts was exported using `New-MailboxExportRequest` and `Get-MailboxExportRequest` (T1114.002, T1586.002), typically limited to recent correspondence. The exported mailbox data was compressed and stored as `C:\ProgramFiles\Microsoft\ExchangeServer\V15\FrontEnd\HttpProxy\owa\auth\Redir.png` , while the user temp directory was archived as `exfil.png`. Both files were staged for exfiltration using HTTP requests (T1005, T1071.001, T1074.002, T1048.002). Password-protected archives (T1560.001) further protected the exfiltrated content. After exfiltration, the attacker removed export request evidence using Remove-MailboxExportRequest (T1070.008). APT29 has been observed compressing and encrypting stolen data before transmission and utilizing encrypted, non-C2 channels to evade detection [76, 71].

4.9.3 APT37

APT37, also known as InkySquid, ScarCruft, or Reaper, is a North Korean state-sponsored APT group active since at least 2012. The group is primarily focused on cyber-espionage against South Korean targets, but its operations have also affected a range of global entities [78].

4.9.3.1 Initial Access

APT37 is notable for its use of sophisticated initial access techniques, including browser exploits, spear-phishing, and supply chain attacks. The group regularly delivers payloads via malicious documents and compromised websites [79]. In one documented campaign, APT37 exploited a vulnerability in Internet Explorer (CVE-2020-1380) (T1203), enabling drive-by compromise (T1189) without user interaction. The attacker sent a phishing email containing a malicious link; when opened, the target was redirected to an attacker-controlled site which exploited IE by loading additional JavaScript. This JavaScript decoded a final SVG variable, resulting in a blob containing a hex-encoded Cobalt Strike stager (T1027), which utilized HTTPS for C2 (T1071.001) and was subsequently decoded and executed on the victim's machine [79]. Most of the code appeared benign, aiding evasion during both automated and manual analysis.

4.9.3.2 Execution and Payload Delivery

The attacker used the Cobalt Strike beacon command line (T1059.003) to install (T1105) Python 2.7 on the victim's system and schedule a Python script (T1053.005, T1059.006) that loaded a Bluelight sample

[6]SHA256: cb80a074e5fde8d297c2c74a0377e612b4030cc756baf4fff3cc2452ebc04a9c

(replaced with Cobalt Strike beacon due to the unavailability of Bluelight, and later with Meterpreter in subsequent weeks). Afterwards, Ruby 2.7 was installed and a scheduled task (T1053.005) was created to execute a Ruby script (T1059) that ran a RokRAT loader PE file. APT37's primary backdoor, RokRAT[7], provides comprehensive remote access capabilities, including keylogging, screenshot capture, command execution, and process discovery (T1057). RokRAT is injected into `cmd.exe` (T1055) and utilizes API calls such as VirtualAlloc(), WriteProcessMemory(), and CreateRemoteThread() for process injection (T1106). The group also employs steganography, sending images with embedded shellcode to victims (T1027.003). RokRAT's newer versions have introduced advanced anti-analysis and stealth features [80, 81].

4.9.3.3 Discovery and Credential Access

After establishing access, APT37 used browserStealer to collect user-saved passwords from browsers (T1555.003). The group performed further system discovery using commands such as `hostname` and `set`, retrieved BIOS information via registry queries (T1082), and ran multiple `cmd` commands to identify system owners and active users (T1033).

4.9.3.4 Persistence

APT37 ensures continued access by registering scheduled tasks and modifying registry keys (`HKCU:\Software\Microsoft\Windows\CurrentVersion\Run`) to automatically launch malware at system startup (T1547.001, T1053.005). Additionally, the group leverages legitimate cloud services for command-and-control communication, complicating detection and blocking efforts [81].

4.9.3.5 Data Collection and Exfiltration

File exfiltration is a core objective for APT37 (T1005). The group actively seeks files with extensions such as .doc, .pdf, and .txt, aggregates them into a zip archive within a staging directory on the compromised system, and exfiltrates the archive using Dropbox (T1567.002).

4.9.4 Patchwork

Patchwork is a cyber-espionage group first observed in December 2015. While definitive attribution is lacking, evidence suggests a likely pro-Indian or Indian nexus. Patchwork has focused on diplomatic and government targets and has previously conducted spear-phishing campaigns against U.S. think tank groups [82]. Recent research from Cyble Research and Intelligence Labs (CRIL) highlights campaigns targeting Chinese entities, consistent with Patchwork's historic operations [83].

4.9.4.1 Initial Access

In a recent campaign, Patchwork initiated infection using a specially crafted LNK file, typically delivered to victims through targeted phishing emails (T1660). When the user executed the LNK file (T1204), it launched

[7] SHA256: 9b383ebc1c592d5556fec9d513223d4f99a5061591671db560faf742dd68493f

a PowerShell script (T1059.001) designed to retrieve two files from attacker-controlled infrastructure, specifically, from the domains `jihang[.]scapematic[.]info` and `shianchi[.]scapematic[.]info`. The first file downloaded is a PDF, which acts as a user lure (T1036.008, T1024.002); the second is a malicious DLL payload. The PowerShell script first saves the PDF as `C:\ProgramData\186523.pdf`, which is often empty and designed solely for social engineering. Next, it downloads the malicious DLL with an initial name such as `hal`, storing it in the same directory (`C:\ProgramData\hal`). Immediately after downloading, the script renames this file to `wer.dll` (`C:\ProgramData\wer.dll`) to prepare for the sideloading stage.
All network transmissions for these downloads are conducted over HTTPS, but use self-signed certificates to evade detection and leverage encrypted channels (T1587.002, T1553.002). A representative LNK sample from this campaign is "186523-pdf.lnk"[8], while the corresponding DLL payload is identified by SHA256 hash [9] [84]. By carefully orchestrating these downloads and renames, Patchwork prepares the environment for subsequent DLL sideloading, enabling the attack chain to proceed with stealth and persistence.

4.9.4.2 Execution, Sideloading, and Defense Evasion

The script copies the legitimate Windows system file "WerFaultSecure.exe" from `C:\Windows\System32` to `C:\ProgramData`, a step used to enable DLL sideloading (T1574.002). It then schedules a task named "EdgeUpdate" to regularly execute this binary (T1053.005), ensuring persistence. "WerFaultSecure.exe" sideloads the malicious DLL, which decrypts and injects shellcode directly into the WerFaultSecure process memory (T1055). The injected shellcode patches the AmsiScanBuffer, AmsiScanString, and EtwEventWrite APIs to evade AMSI and Microsoft's event tracing (defense evasion). After patching, the shellcode creates a section object from previously decrypted content and maps it into the WerFaultSecure address space, allowing the final VC++ compiled payload to execute in-memory, undetected. Using the `LoadLibraryW()` API, the malware loads necessary modules. A mutex named "dsds" is created to ensure only one malware instance runs at a time, then the console window is hidden and the malware continues running in the background.

4.9.4.3 Discovery and System Information Gathering

The malware uses `GetAdaptersInfo()` and `GetHostName()` to gather network adapter and device name details (T1082). It queries the victim's public IP address from an external service[10] using a specific user agent. After collecting system details including process ID, local and public IP addresses, Windows version, username, MAC address, and a hardcoded user-agent string (T1033), the malware computes the SHA256 hash for these values, encodes it in Base64, and passes it through a Salsa20 encryption algorithm with another Base64 encoding step (T1132.001). The resulting encrypted data is transmitted via HTTP POST to the Patchwork C&C server[11] (T1071).

---

[8] SHA256: d7b278d20f47203da07c33f646844e74cb690ed802f2ba27a74e216368df7db9
[9] SHA256: ba262c587f1f5df7c2ab763434ef80785c5b51cac861774bf66d579368b56e31
[10] `https://myexternalip.com/raw`
[11] `Iceandfire[.]xyz`

4.9.4.4 C&C Communication and Malicious Tasking

After transmitting data to the C&C, the malware creates two threads for further malicious activities. These threads read the server's response and compare it with keywords such as `upload`, `uplexe`, `download`, `filelist`, and `screenshot` (T1041), enabling file transfer, execution, directory listing, and screenshot capture on the victim host.

4.9.4.5 Persistence and Additional Backdoors

Persistence is maintained by the scheduled "EdgeUpdate" task (T1053.005) and by malware such as Unknown Logger, which writes its application path to `SOFTWARE\Microsoft\Windows\CurrentVersion\Run` in the registry (T1547.001) [85]. Unknown Logger is a public free backdoor capable of browser credential theft (T1555), keylogging (T1056.001), screenshot capture, lateral movement, and downloading/executing secondary malware. It sends stolen keystrokes over SMTP and can be used to download and run Metasploit Meterpreter via its `DownloadExecFileURL` configuration. This configuration enables remote download and execution of additional payloads, such as Meterpreter.

4.9.4.6 Post-Exploitation, Lateral Movement, and Final Payloads

Metasploit Meterpreter is used for C2 and system discovery via a reverse HTTPS shell [85, 86], executing commands such as `getuid`, `sysinfo`, `ipconfig`, and `route`. Subsequently, a QuasarRAT binary named `microsoft_network.exe` is downloaded to the victim system (T1036.005) and used as a final exfiltration tool (T1105) [87, 88].

QuasarRAT is an open-source (T1588.002) C# remote access tool distributed via GitHub, providing AES-encrypted communications, file management (download/upload/execute), keylogging, remote desktop, webcam access, reverse shell (T1059.003), and credential recovery from browsers and FTP clients. QuasarRAT uses non-standard ports (such as 4782) for TCP callbacks (T1571), can determine host geolocation (T1614), and schedules a "Microsoft_Security_Task" to ensure persistence at user logon (T1053.005). The RAT recursively searches for files matching specified extensions (e.g., *.doc, *.docx, *.xls, *.xlsx, *.pdf, *.ppt, *.pptx, *.eml, *.msg, *.rtf, *.csv) (T1083) [88, 86, 85], and exfiltrates them with its file manager utility (T1005, T1119).

4.9.5 Sandworm

Sandworm Team is a destructive threat group attributed to Russia's General Staff Main Intelligence Directorate (GRU) Main Center for Special Technologies (GTsST), military unit 74455, and has been active since at least 2009 [89]. The group is notorious for high-profile operations such as the 2015–2016 attacks on Ukrainian power infrastructure, the global 2017 NotPetya campaign, the 2018 Olympic Destroyer incident, and intrusions targeting the 2017 French presidential election and international organizations, sometimes with support from GRU Unit 26165 (APT28) [89].

Sponsored by Russian military intelligence, Sandworm (also tracked as APT44) is operationally mature and integrates espionage, destructive attack, and information operations as part of Russia's broader doctrine of "information confrontation" [26]. APT44 has aggressively pursued a multi-pronged strategy to support Russia's military and political objectives. Throughout Russia's war in Ukraine, APT44 has waged intense campaigns of cyber sabotage, leveraging disruptive malware (especially wipers) to impact a wide range of critical infrastructure, often in tandem with conventional military operations. As the war has continued, the group's focus has increasingly shifted toward intelligence collection and exfiltration to provide battlefield advantage to Russian forces [26]. For example, one APT44 campaign aided forward-deployed Russian troops by exfiltrating communications from captured mobile devices to process relevant targeting data. APT44's approach to supporting the military campaign has evolved significantly over the past two years.

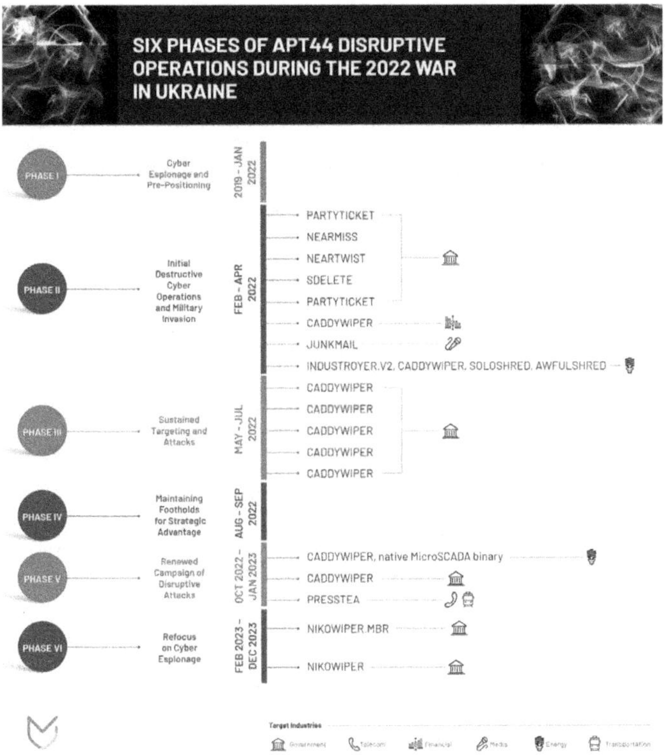

Figure 39: APT44's wartime disruptive activity [26]

In late 2022, Mandiant responded to a multi-stage cyber-physical incident in which Sandworm targeted a Ukrainian critical infrastructure organization [90]. The attack leveraged novel techniques for impacting industrial control systems (ICS) and operational technology (OT), using OT-level living off the land (LotL) techniques to likely trip the victim's substation circuit breakers, causing an unplanned power outage that coincided with mass missile strikes across Ukraine. Sandworm subsequently conducted a second disruptive event by deploying a new variant of CADDYWIPER[12] in the victim's IT environment [91]. The techniques leveraged during the incident indicate a growing maturity of Russia's OT attack arsenal, including an ability to rapidly recognize novel OT threat vectors, develop new capabilities, and adapt attacks to different types of OT infrastructure [90, 92].

4.9.5.1 Initial Access and Delivery

The initial compromise was achieved through a phishing email directly attaching a ZIP archive named `confidential.zip`, exploiting CVE-2023-38831 [93]. The archive included both a decoy PDF document and a malicious BAT file designed to execute the Rhadamanthys infostealer[13], a commodity info-stealer capable of collecting and exfiltrating browser credentials (T1539), session data, and broader system information (T1082, T0872, T1105) [94, 95]. Rhadamanthys operates on a subscription model and is rarely used by state actors, making its appearance in this campaign notable [93].

4.9.5.2 Initial Compromise and Maintaining Presence

Based on analysis, the intrusion began on or prior to June 2022 and culminated in two disruptive events on October 10 and 12, 2022 [90]. Sandworm was first observed in the victim's environment when the group deployed the Neo-REGEORG webshell on an internet-facing server, reflecting a technique seen in their previous campaigns. About a month later, Sandworm deployed the GOGETTER tunneler (a Golang proxy utilizing Yamux over TLS for C2 traffic, T1095, T1572). Persistence was maintained using scheduled tasks (Task Scheduler on Windows, replacing the observed initially Systemd approach), with attackers repeatedly testing and correcting scheduled task paths to ensure reliable C2 reconnection after restarts (T1036.004, T1543.002).

4.9.5.3 Lateral Movement and ICS/OT Intrusion

Sandworm moved laterally to access the hypervisor hosting a SCADA management instance for the victim's substation. The attackers likely maintained access to the SCADA system for up to three months. For the OT phase, attackers downloaded a malicious ISO file (`a.iso`) using `certutil` to both user and admin directories. The ISO was mounted (via PowerShell and Windows utilities) and contained:

- `lun.vbs` – a Visual Basic script to invoke further execution,
- `n.bat` – a batch script launching the payload,
- `s1.txt` – a file likely containing unauthorized MicroSCADA control commands.

The system was configured to autorun inserted ISO images (T0847, T0895). The reconstructed execution chain included:

[12] SHA256: a294620543334a721a2ae8eaaf9680a0786f4b9a216d75b55cfd28f39e9430ea

[13] SHA256: bb8bbcc948e8dca2e5a0270c41c062a29994a2d9b51e820ed74d9b6e2a01ddcf

- `wscript.exe "d:\pack\lun.vbs"` (T1059.005)
- `cmd /c "d:\pack\n.bat"` (T0853)

In the original incident, the batch file (`n.bat`) would launch the native MicroSCADA binary (`scilc.exe`) with the `-do` flag and `s1.txt` as a SCIL program. To mimic attacker behavior, our simulation instead ran a Python script reading and executing commands from `s1.txt`, emulating the impact of SCIL logic (T0871, T0855, T0807, T0831, T0894). The MicroSCADA system was End-of-Life and allowed default access to the SCIL-API, and SCIL commands are capable of operating substation RTUs via both IEC-60870-5-104 (TCP/IP) and IEC-60870-5-101 (serial). Although the actual commands executed were unrecoverable, they were likely used to trip substation circuit breakers and cause an unplanned outage [90].

4.9.5.4 Destructive Payload Deployment

Two days after executing the OT event, Sandworm deployed a new variant of CADDYWIPER [91, 92], a C-based wiper focused on irrecoverably destroying data by overwriting files, mapped drives, and eventually the physical partition (T0872, T1485, T0809). CADDYWIPER was staged as `caddywiper.exe` and deployed network-wide using Group Policy Objects (GPO), with instructions to copy the executable from a staging server to endpoint local disks (T1570, T1484.001). Execution was coordinated via the TANKTRAP PowerShell utility (T1059.001), which utilized GPOs to schedule and trigger wiper execution at a set time (T1053.005). This method has also been seen used to distribute other disruptive tools such as NEARMISS, SDELETE, and PARTYTICKET.
Multiple GPO updates (`gpupdate`) were performed and tasks retried across endpoints as needed to ensure effective delivery and coverage. The wiper campaign focused on making data irrecoverable and maximizing operational disruption, but did not impact the hypervisor or SCADA VM, possibly due to operational error or team segmentation. In several cases, failures or incomplete coverage required manual remediation on key systems such as domain controllers.

4.9.6 Magic Hound

Magic Hound is an Iranian-sponsored threat group (also tracked as APT35 or Charming Kitten) known for long-term, resource-intensive cyber operations targeting government, military, academic, and international organizations [96]. This group frequently leverages Microsoft Exchange vulnerabilities, such as the ProxyShell chain (CVE-2021-34473, CVE-2021-34523, CVE-2021-31207), to gain SYSTEM-level code execution on Exchange servers [97] (T1190).

4.9.6.1 Initial Access and Web Shell Deployment

In our experiments, prior to exploitation, we performed vulnerability scanning with Metasploit to identify Exchange servers susceptible to ProxyShell (T1595.002). Initial access was then achieved by exploiting the ProxyShell vulnerability chain (CVE-2021-34473, CVE-2021-34523, CVE-2021-31207) on the target Exchange server, granting SYSTEM-level command execution (T1190, T1078.001, T1071.00). As part of this exploitation, we issued mailbox export requests (T1114.002) and subsequently removed them to cover tracks (T1070.003), reflecting steps documented in actual Magic Hound campaigns [97].

After successful exploitation, we deployed multiple web shells (e.g., `login.aspx`, randomly-named .aspx files) to directories resembling legitimate OWA/Exchange locations (T1505.003, T1036.004, T1036.005). Using these shells, we performed reconnaissance via commands such as `ipconfig /all`, `hostname`, `ping`, `systeminfo`, `nltest`, `nbtstat`, `arp -a`, `net user`, and `query user` to enumerate the network, host configuration, and domain information (T1087.003, T1059.003, T1482, T1018, T1047).

4.9.6.2 Account Manipulation and Privilege Escalation

Leveraging SYSTEM-level privileges provided by ProxyShell, we enabled the built-in `DefaultAccount`, set its password, and added it to the `Administrators` and `Remote Desktop Users` groups using PowerShell commands via the web shell (T1098.007, T1059.001, T1136.001, T1036.010). This procedure directly mirrors techniques used by Magic Hound adversaries to maintain access and escalate privileges [97]. After enabling `DefaultAccount`, we used RDP to connect to the Exchange mail server with admin rights for subsequent operations (T1021.001, T1078.001).

4.9.6.3 Remote Access Tunneling and Persistence

To enable RDP connectivity from the internet, `plink.exe` (PuTTY Link) was uploaded and run from the compromised Exchange server to establish an SSH tunnel back to attacker-controlled infrastructure, exposing RDP externally via a forwarded port (T1572, T1588.002). After RDP connectivity was confirmed, the next step was to transfer tooling for further post-exploitation (T1105).

For persistence and covert RDP tunneling, we uploaded `CacheTask.zip` via the web shell, then unarchived it and ran its contents using the same web shell interface (not via RDP) (T1105, T1036.004, T1036.005). The archive contained several files: `CacheTask.bat`, `CacheTask.xml`, `dllhost.exe` (the renamed Fast Reverse Proxy [FRP] binary), `RuntimeBroker` (FRP configuration), and `install-proxy.bat`. Running `install-proxy.bat` created new directories for the payloads, moved files into place, deleted any prior scheduled task named `CacheTask`, then registered and started a new scheduled task for persistence and covert channel establishment (T1053.005, T1090). `CacheTask.bat` repeatedly invoked the FRP binary, ensuring a reliable tunnel over HTTP [97] (T1071.00). To further obscure its function, the FRP tunneling binary was renamed `dllhost.exe` (T1036.005).

4.9.6.4 Credential Access and Internal Reconnaissance

Once interactive access was established, we used Task Manager on the compromised server to dump the LSASS process. We extracted the memory dump for credential harvesting (T1003.001, T1560.001, T1005), in line with methods reported in real incidents. We also leveraged the new administrative access to query domain controllers and other internal hosts for further information, and in several cases, used Impacket's `wmiexec.py` utility to directly execute commands on the domain controller from the mail server (T1059.003, T1059.001).

4.9.6.5 Lateral Movement and Tool Deployment

After connecting to the Exchange mail server using `DefaultAccount` and RDP, we continued with lateral movement to internal assets, including workstations, domain controllers, and application servers. RDP was primarily used for these connections, leveraging the credentials obtained via LSASS dumping or previously enabled accounts (T1021.001, T1078.002, T1570). In some experiments, we also used `wmiexec.py` from the mail server to deploy payloads to the domain controller, varying our approach to increase dataset diversity (T1047, T1105). The tools used for deployment were `setup.bat` (a batch script for server-side encryption and configuration) and `dcrypt.exe` (the DiskCryptor utility for workstation encryption). In deploying these payloads, we experimented with various combinations and paths: copying via RDP, running from the desktop or system directories, and executing as administrator to simulate real-world variability (T1105).

4.9.6.6 Impact and System Modification

For the destructive phase, we replicated Magic Hound's actions by deploying both `setup.bat` and DiskCryptor's `dcrypt.exe` to the targeted hosts (T1486). `setup.bat` was designed to disable the Windows event log service, enable BitLocker and RDP, prepare the system drive for encryption (using `BdeHdCfg`), trigger the encryption process, restart the system, modify registry keys as part of BitLocker and RDP setup (T1112), and self-delete upon completion (T1562.002, T1562.004, T1070.003, T1070.004). DiskCryptor installation required a reboot to install its kernel driver and a subsequent reboot to encrypt and lock the workstation fully. In our experiments, we varied the deployment of `setup.bat` and `dcrypt.exe` across different scenarios and machines, sometimes deploying both to servers and workstations in various combinations to introduce diversity to the dataset. In contrast, in real-world Magic Hound operations, the attacker typically deploys `setup.bat` to servers and `dcrypt.exe` (DiskCryptor) to workstations [97]. These actions rendered the target systems inaccessible, consistent with destructive impacts observed in documented Magic Hound campaigns.

4.9.6.7 Defense Evasion and Masquerading

We followed defense evasion tactics described in public incident reports: web shells were placed in locations matching legitimate OWA login pages (T1036.004, T1505.003), and the FRP tunneling binary was renamed `dllhost.exe` to mask its true purpose (T1036.005). The scheduled task was given a benign name (`CacheTask`) to blend in with legitimate Windows tasks (T1036.004). Such masquerading techniques are commonly observed in Magic Hound intrusions [97].

Table 7: APT Attack Techniques by Group

Group	#Tech	MITRE Techniques	Description
FIN7	33	T1190, T1059.001, T1564.003, T1620, T1571, T1033, T1588.002, T1588.003, T1069.002, T1072, T1059.003, T1105, T1087.002, T1082, T1497.001, T1218.011, T1057, T1486, T1055, T1573.002, T1071.001, T1132.001, T1105, T1114.002, T1072.010, T1069.002, T1547.001, T1055, T1070.004, T1083, T1082, T1036	Exploit MailServer — enumerate domain entities — send powershell loader to deploy encoded CS — Kerberoasting — run powerplant as backdoor — send reconnaissance tools — Blackmatter Ransomware
APT29	30	T1021.001, T1566.001, T1204.002, T1078, T1133, T1589, T1078.002, T1078.003, T1105, T1087.002, T1083, T1059.003, T1036.005, T1036.004, T1586.002, T1114.002, T1560.001, T1055, T1071.001, T1074.002, T1048.002, T1070.008, T1070.004, T1059.001, T1053.005, T1587.001, T1071, T1070, T1562, T1555	Rogue RDP — steal credentials — RDP to mail server/DC — deploy Caldera — Steal Chrome Cookies — Change Firewall Rules — Schedule Task to launch Malware — Account/Domain Discovery using Adfind — Export users Mailboxes — Compress data before exfiltration — download compressed files from public URLs
APT37	19	T1106, T1055, T1027.003, T1057, T1203, T1189, T1027, T1071.001, T1059.003, T1105, T1053.005, T1059.006, T1059, T1555.003, T1082, T1033, T1547.001, T1005, T1567.002	Exploit Internet Explorer/Deploy CS — Download/Install Ruby/Python — Schedule Ruby/Python Tasks — Steal Firefox passwords — system discovery — Take Screenshot — Find/Compress Files with extensions — Exfiltrate to Dropbox
Patchwork	23	T1660, T1059.001, T1036.008, T1024.002, T1574.002, T1055, T1082, T1132.001, T1033, T1071, T1041, T1547.001, T1056.001, T1588.002, T1571, T1614, T1059.003, T1036.005, T1105, T1083, T1105, T1119, T1053.005	Phishing LNK — Keylogger+Meterpreter — side load — network discovery — Elevate Access — DLL injection — Schedule Task — Quasar RAT — Search/Obtain File Extensions — Download/Exfil Files
Sandworm	24	T1484.001, T1059.001, T1053.005, T0872, T1105, T1539, T1082, T1095, T1572, T1543.002, T1036.004, T0847, T0895, T0871, T1059.005, T0853, T0855, T0894, T0831, T0872, T1485, T0809, T1570, T1053.005	Exploit WinRAR — go-getter backdoor — Schedule Task — Mount iso — Add GPO Task in DC — CaddyWiper
Magic Hound	35	T1190, T1595.002, T1505.003, T1036.004, T1036.005, T1071.00, T1087.003, T1059.003, T1482, T1018, T1047, T1098.007, T1059.001, T1136.001, T1036.010, T1021.001, T1572, T1588.002, T1105, T1053.005, T1090, T1560.001, T1005, T1003.001, T1078.002, T1570, T1114.002, T1070.003, T1486, T1562.002, T1562.004, T1070.004, T1112	Exploit Exchange Server — deploy multiple web shells — Check Port — domain/network/system discovery — enable RDP/firewall — enable and add DefaultAccount to privileged groups — Scheduled Task for HTTP-based C2 — Plink for tunneling/RDP — Dump lsass — dump and exfil LSASS for credentials — move laterally via RDP and WMI — use BitLocker and DiskCryptor for encryption

5 Experiments and Results

5.1 Graph Construction and Labeling

Table 8 summarizes the dataset building process and node-level labeling across all days, APT groups, and machines. For each machine log, we report the total number of unique events, the number of events retained for graph construction, and the number of events skipped. The skipped events correspond to records that did not contribute meaningful context for attack analysis or did not enrich the provenance structure. In practice, the goal was to preserve as much information as possible in the provenance graphs, while filtering only those events that would not affect downstream detection or attribution. The table further shows the resulting graph size in terms of nodes and edges, together with the number of nodes labeled as malicious before and after applying whitelisting rules.

The totals in the last row provide a global overview of the dataset. Across all logs, 282,474,445 unique events were recorded, of which 278,225,840 were processed into graphs, while 4,248,605 were skipped. These events resulted in 32,412,413 nodes connected by 103,879,244 edges. Before applying whitelisting, 331,450 nodes were labeled as malicious, which corresponds to about 1.02% of all nodes. After whitelisting, the number of malicious nodes was reduced to 27,310, or 0.084% of all nodes. This represents a reduction of 304,140 nodes, meaning that 91.76% of the originally flagged malicious nodes were excluded by whitelisting. This aggressive reduction highlights both the necessity of labeling refinement and the importance of maintaining high precision in downstream attribution.

Table 8: Graph construction and labeling statistics per day, APT group, and machine. Columns list: Day, APT Group, Machine, number of unique events in logs, number of events used to construct the graph, number of events skipped, number of nodes, number of edges, number of nodes labeled malicious before whitelisting, and number of nodes labeled malicious after applying whitelisting.

Day	APT Group	Machine	Events	Used	Skipped	Nodes	Edges	Mal nodes	Whitelisted
2025-04-09	FIN7	DESKTOP-WIN10	295118	293823	1295	13077	49575	0	0
2025-04-09	FIN7	DESKTOP-WIN11	745382	734614	10768	39262	178849	0	0
2025-04-09	FIN7	SERVER-MAIL	2186205	2093131	93074	181269	545852	391	267
2025-04-09	FIN7	SERVER-WEB	127890	124337	3553	6866	34542	0	0
2025-04-09	FIN7	WIN-5166H0VRQLS	2512121	2466630	45491	149068	1042165	0	0
2025-04-09	FIN7	WIN-PORTAL	2573135	2565148	7987	281560	592841	0	0
2025-04-10	APT29	DESKTOP-WIN10	326759	325493	1266	21615	57464	3	3
2025-04-10	APT29	DESKTOP-WIN11	779663	770790	8873	199488	337239	3	3
2025-04-10	APT29	SERVER-MAIL	1806915	1732958	73957	155508	474883	358	108
2025-04-10	APT29	SERVER-WEB	167965	162271	5694	14317	45816	0	0
2025-04-10	APT29	WIN-5166H0VRQLS	2245253	2202786	42467	131241	908828	0	0
2025-04-10	APT29	WIN-PORTAL	119479	117476	2003	15289	50579	0	0
2025-04-11	APT37	DESKTOP-WIN10	393822	391811	2011	91238	189856	50775	268
2025-04-11	APT37	DESKTOP-WIN11	627445	622319	5126	202482	318692	0	0
2025-04-11	APT37	SERVER-MAIL	2308139	2232779	75360	199536	609861	0	0
2025-04-11	APT37	SERVER-WEB	77494	74279	3215	5596	29003	0	0

Continued on next page

Day	APT Group	Machine	#Events	Used	Skipped	Nodes	Edges	Mal nodes	Whitelisted
2025-04-11	APT37	WIN-5166H0VRQLS	2254058	2213729	40329	167736	982581	0	0
2025-04-11	APT37	WIN-PORTAL	103823	100206	3617	14137	42204	0	0
2025-04-12	Patchwork	DESKTOP-WIN10	173986	172856	1130	11608	44551	0	0
2025-04-12	Patchwork	DESKTOP-WIN11	1271357	1264458	6899	106049	538174	4653	3603
2025-04-12	Patchwork	SERVER-MAIL	2516949	2450120	66829	220477	673243	0	0
2025-04-12	Patchwork	SERVER-WEB	95900	93064	2836	5324	28318	0	0
2025-04-12	Patchwork	WIN-5166H0VRQLS	2330920	2293374	37546	143185	997046	0	0
2025-04-12	Patchwork	WIN-PORTAL	138374	135333	3041	13160	52159	0	0
2025-04-13	Benign	DESKTOP-WIN10	295494	294436	1058	24916	93852	0	0
2025-04-13	Benign	DESKTOP-WIN11	1614804	1607864	6940	221055	465900	0	0
2025-04-13	Benign	SERVER-MAIL	2732574	2678116	54458	255796	783338	0	0
2025-04-13	Benign	SERVER-WEB	116905	115127	1778	7604	35070	0	0
2025-04-13	Benign	WIN-5166H0VRQLS	2657465	2622588	34877	161293	1156194	0	0
2025-04-13	Benign	WIN-PORTAL	189002	186806	2196	14995	63386	0	0
2025-04-14	Sandworm	DESKTOP-WIN10	244695	242800	1895	21291	65794	16	7
2025-04-14	Sandworm	DESKTOP-WIN11	1324460	1319504	4956	79292	313944	9	4
2025-04-14	Sandworm	SERVER-MAIL	2295530	2248031	47499	208215	641904	10	5
2025-04-14	Sandworm	SERVER-WEB	78406	77231	1175	3101	23411	0	0
2025-04-14	Sandworm	WIN-5166H0VRQLS	2601575	2571664	29911	158544	1091223	230	139
2025-04-14	Sandworm	WIN-PORTAL	156682	154967	1715	13203	60398	12	5
2025-04-15	MagicHound	DESKTOP-WIN10	435469	418601	16868	41715	121058	25	23
2025-04-15	MagicHound	DESKTOP-WIN11	1545791	1534227	11564	241026	797311	144	118
2025-04-15	MagicHound	SERVER-MAIL	2018964	1950127	68837	191581	553949	221	137
2025-04-15	MagicHound	SERVER-WEB	265015	261280	3735	24973	81881	79	56
2025-04-15	MagicHound	WIN-5166H0VRQLS	1922343	1891983	30360	122175	830899	1	1
2025-04-15	MagicHound	WIN-PORTAL	159638	155373	4265	21101	57829	0	0
2025-04-16	FIN7	DESKTOP-WIN10	338045	333875	4170	35015	105812	0	0
2025-04-16	FIN7	DESKTOP-WIN11	2030587	2013472	17115	393058	861039	0	0
2025-04-16	FIN7	SERVER-MAIL	3965601	3895945	69656	453689	1179726	433	291
2025-04-16	FIN7	SERVER-WEB	97745	95767	1978	9842	35195	0	0
2025-04-16	FIN7	WIN-5166H0VRQLS	2591541	2551549	39992	386188	1252831	0	0
2025-04-16	FIN7	WIN-PORTAL	777522	773482	4040	86750	218445	0	0
2025-04-17	APT37	DESKTOP-WIN10	504692	500401	4291	169972	260680	99645	255
2025-04-17	APT37	DESKTOP-WIN11	1508068	1505346	2722	158229	560952	0	0
2025-04-17	APT37	SERVER-MAIL	2305283	2262123	43160	196221	539913	0	0
2025-04-17	APT37	SERVER-WEB	148980	147599	1381	13280	48040	0	0
2025-04-17	APT37	WIN-5166H0VRQLS	2077790	2064766	13024	155511	1079878	0	0
2025-04-17	APT37	WIN-PORTAL	164634	161864	2770	15735	61071	0	0
2025-04-18	Sandworm	DESKTOP-WIN10	262543	258512	4031	23859	80136	17	6
2025-04-18	Sandworm	DESKTOP-WIN11	1170011	1167945	2066	155644	466656	10	6
2025-04-18	Sandworm	SERVER-MAIL	1813080	1777281	35799	159316	433502	0	0
2025-04-18	Sandworm	SERVER-WEB	225585	224093	1492	12550	53105	0	0
2025-04-18	Sandworm	WIN-5166H0VRQLS	2308304	2265327	42977	140437	986018	132	81
2025-04-18	Sandworm	WIN-PORTAL	241472	238393	3079	47716	114795	18	7
2025-04-19	MagicHound	DESKTOP-WIN10	465414	460990	4424	56424	152750	83	59

Continued on next page

Day	APT Group	Machine	#Events	Used	Skipped	Nodes	Edges	Mal nodes	Whitelisted
2025-04-19	MagicHound	DESKTOP-WIN11	1974346	1971269	3077	179323	573534	81	57
2025-04-19	MagicHound	SERVER-MAIL	2083228	2028175	55053	187015	510586	6716	268
2025-04-19	MagicHound	SERVER-WEB	91767	90512	1255	5075	31297	0	0
2025-04-19	MagicHound	WIN-5166H0VRQLS	2116417	2064472	51945	127450	927137	0	0
2025-04-19	MagicHound	WIN-PORTAL	314087	309978	4109	26372	110934	81	53
2025-04-20	Benign	DESKTOP-WIN10	333966	330318	3648	40118	109149	0	0
2025-04-20	Benign	DESKTOP-WIN11	1638869	1634938	3931	156798	499591	0	0
2025-04-20	Benign	SERVER-MAIL	2336325	2292737	43588	208721	558932	0	0
2025-04-20	Benign	SERVER-WEB	129496	128098	1398	15443	46158	0	0
2025-04-20	Benign	WIN-5166H0VRQLS	2613944	2580409	33535	162337	1135905	0	0
2025-04-20	Benign	WIN-PORTAL	196456	193401	3055	20008	74778	0	0
2025-04-21	Patchwork	DESKTOP-WIN10	296990	293634	3356	21555	85452	0	0
2025-04-21	Patchwork	DESKTOP-WIN11	2316085	2311945	4140	186346	973996	5640	4386
2025-04-21	Patchwork	SERVER-MAIL	1835850	1775378	60472	157815	433732	0	0
2025-04-21	Patchwork	SERVER-WEB	91658	89696	1962	4639	30885	0	0
2025-04-21	Patchwork	WIN-5166H0VRQLS	2001281	1969049	32232	121521	865538	0	0
2025-04-21	Patchwork	WIN-PORTAL	157248	153658	3590	13619	60607	0	0
2025-04-22	APT29	DESKTOP-WIN10	327379	324232	3147	27166	105102	2	2
2025-04-22	APT29	DESKTOP-WIN11	1344464	1339559	4905	170222	509934	2	2
2025-04-22	APT29	SERVER-MAIL	2207780	2135182	72598	195158	538707	351	96
2025-04-22	APT29	SERVER-WEB	129564	128362	1202	9164	38754	0	0
2025-04-22	APT29	WIN-5166H0VRQLS	2474876	2429685	45191	152845	1082668	111	54
2025-04-22	APT29	WIN-PORTAL	157656	155429	2227	14291	56783	0	0
2025-04-23	Sandworm	DESKTOP-WIN10	219966	213988	5978	32134	59880	17	6
2025-04-23	Sandworm	DESKTOP-WIN11	743148	739020	4128	190317	391583	10	6
2025-04-23	Sandworm	SERVER-MAIL	1298115	1272481	25634	115966	311309	0	0
2025-04-23	Sandworm	SERVER-WEB	51619	50015	1604	3387	23531	0	0
2025-04-23	Sandworm	WIN-5166H0VRQLS	2370341	2229460	140881	132371	943763	254	157
2025-04-23	Sandworm	WIN-PORTAL	259318	255743	3575	78982	109235	15	6
2025-04-24	Patchwork	DESKTOP-WIN10	349031	345750	3281	31754	103873	0	0
2025-04-24	Patchwork	DESKTOP-WIN11	1966191	1957694	8497	196176	929383	6423	4990
2025-04-24	Patchwork	SERVER-MAIL	1298115	1272481	25634	183261	498291	0	0
2025-04-24	Patchwork	SERVER-WEB	187759	185797	1962	15523	66485	0	0
2025-04-24	Patchwork	WIN-5166H0VRQLS	2367285	2337092	30193	140255	997318	0	0
2025-04-24	Patchwork	WIN-PORTAL	298054	294580	3474	39758	127272	0	0
2025-04-25	MagicHound	DESKTOP-WIN10	506053	500572	5481	67612	173648	94	85
2025-04-25	MagicHound	DESKTOP-WIN11	1792653	1780571	12082	189205	568724	2	2
2025-04-25	MagicHound	SERVER-MAIL	2276791	2215560	61231	223884	594371	6499	132
2025-04-25	MagicHound	SERVER-WEB	198323	196841	1482	10347	47331	0	0
2025-04-25	MagicHound	WIN-5166H0VRQLS	2305004	2248610	56394	143641	990134	0	0
2025-04-25	MagicHound	WIN-PORTAL	300171	291402	8769	36062	105425	0	0
2025-04-26	FIN7	DESKTOP-WIN10	297203	292516	4687	40255	108257	0	0
2025-04-26	FIN7	DESKTOP-WIN11	1239057	1232596	6461	179646	508666	0	0
2025-04-26	FIN7	SERVER-MAIL	2020330	1981888	38442	193273	511891	359	259
2025-04-26	FIN7	SERVER-WEB	101362	99437	1925	8392	34980	0	0

Continued on next page

Day	APT Group	Machine	#Events	Used	Skipped	Nodes	Edges	Mal nodes	Whitelisted
2025-04-26	FIN7	WIN-5166H0VRQLS	2186872	2159705	27167	137761	953384	0	0
2025-04-26	FIN7	WIN-PORTAL	230782	224827	5955	23840	90397	0	0
2025-04-27	Benign	DESKTOP-WIN10	426598	418380	8218	44213	146749	0	0
2025-04-27	Benign	DESKTOP-WIN11	2722229	2718548	3681	216450	755992	0	0
2025-04-27	Benign	SERVER-MAIL	2846647	2788547	58100	264692	716527	0	0
2025-04-27	Benign	SERVER-WEB	203722	201561	2161	17198	77824	0	0
2025-04-27	Benign	WIN-5166H0VRQLS	3328074	3285399	42675	203781	1410130	0	0
2025-04-27	Benign	WIN-PORTAL	448811	443196	5615	56388	197444	0	0
2025-04-28	APT29	DESKTOP-WIN10	256790	255078	1712	22067	86427	0	0
2025-04-28	APT29	DESKTOP-WIN11	2806240	2802533	3707	162994	506312	3	3
2025-04-28	APT29	SERVER-MAIL	1346921	1324122	22799	200246	492041	529	95
2025-04-28	APT29	SERVER-WEB	159636	158050	1586	16136	58555	0	0
2025-04-28	APT29	WIN-5166H0VRQLS	1612877	1596333	16544	122492	842142	92	53
2025-04-28	APT29	WIN-PORTAL	297661	292525	5136	17600	79530	0	0
2025-04-29	APT37	DESKTOP-WIN10	285439	283717	1722	95843	152547	49813	168
2025-04-29	APT37	DESKTOP-WIN11	1034082	1031660	2422	146972	350193	0	0
2025-04-29	APT37	SERVER-MAIL	951768	923221	28547	87842	238929	0	0
2025-04-29	APT37	SERVER-WEB	86255	84354	1901	9571	40254	0	0
2025-04-29	APT37	WIN-5166H0VRQLS	1008431	993233	15198	75910	433739	0	0
2025-04-29	APT37	WIN-PORTAL	199940	197402	2538	18342	55966	0	0
2025-04-30	APT37	DESKTOP-WIN10	512390	506538	5852	125496	252552	49513	207
2025-04-30	APT37	DESKTOP-WIN11	2937156	2928002	9154	207869	768014	0	0
2025-04-30	APT37	SERVER-MAIL	2470856	2398777	72079	235209	627057	0	0
2025-04-30	APT37	SERVER-WEB	160210	157056	3154	12947	59152	0	0
2025-04-30	APT37	WIN-5166H0VRQLS	2640071	2602939	37132	158391	1141198	0	0
2025-04-30	APT37	WIN-PORTAL	405993	400293	5700	27198	97959	0	0
2025-05-01	MagicHound	DESKTOP-WIN10	503912	497273	6639	64925	186351	96	87
2025-05-01	MagicHound	DESKTOP-WIN11	1910742	1903665	7077	204817	761778	94	83
2025-05-01	MagicHound	SERVER-MAIL	2699521	2602022	97499	278329	698809	6576	189
2025-05-01	MagicHound	SERVER-WEB	189322	188014	1308	13307	50924	0	0
2025-05-01	MagicHound	WIN-5166H0VRQLS	2142565	2114323	28242	142860	937404	104	74
2025-05-01	MagicHound	WIN-PORTAL	230345	224892	5453	28173	82490	86	57
2025-05-02	FIN7	DESKTOP-WIN10	309849	306283	3566	36031	117954	0	0
2025-05-02	FIN7	DESKTOP-WIN11	1465992	1463359	2633	185973	523004	0	0
2025-05-02	FIN7	SERVER-MAIL	2426579	2361865	64714	228244	607825	377	282
2025-05-02	FIN7	SERVER-WEB	169556	167320	2236	11043	42239	0	0
2025-05-02	FIN7	WIN-5166H0VRQLS	2580448	2530451	49997	151121	1098562	0	0
2025-05-02	FIN7	WIN-PORTAL	240869	233940	6929	18998	95761	0	0
2025-05-03	APT29	DESKTOP-WIN10	247944	244541	3403	29412	95403	0	0
2025-05-03	APT29	DESKTOP-WIN11	1278948	1276730	2218	142568	429972	2	2
2025-05-03	APT29	SERVER-MAIL	2159907	2119745	40162	200907	549954	944	101
2025-05-03	APT29	SERVER-WEB	191107	189678	1429	17738	58680	17	12
2025-05-03	APT29	WIN-5166H0VRQLS	2177553	2149133	28420	139915	968466	91	65
2025-05-03	APT29	WIN-PORTAL	224649	221935	2714	25411	88029	0	0
2025-05-04	Benign	DESKTOP-WIN10	362585	358144	4441	23991	95748	0	0

Continued on next page

Day	APT Group	Machine	#Events	Used	Skipped	Nodes	Edges	Mal nodes	Whitelisted
2025-05-04	Benign	DESKTOP-WIN11	1427917	1424070	3847	164669	545215	0	0
2025-05-04	Benign	SERVER-MAIL	2624873	2577754	47119	229286	635552	0	0
2025-05-04	Benign	SERVER-WEB	324224	321697	2527	29145	100493	0	0
2025-05-04	Benign	WIN-5166H0VRQLS	3177872	3140251	37621	187038	1315524	0	0
2025-05-04	Benign	WIN-PORTAL	218212	215676	2536	16847	77434	0	0
2025-05-05	Patchwork	DESKTOP-WIN10	383536	380033	3503	39072	114277	0	0
2025-05-05	Patchwork	DESKTOP-WIN11	2644556	2634071	10485	210939	1127934	7766	6037
2025-05-05	Patchwork	SERVER-MAIL	2000746	1962405	38341	184570	507689	0	0
2025-05-05	Patchwork	SERVER-WEB	107093	105985	1108	7408	38744	0	0
2025-05-05	Patchwork	WIN-5166H0VRQLS	2247569	2203708	43861	130880	931374	0	0
2025-05-05	Patchwork	WIN-PORTAL	336162	331161	5001	24351	96680	0	0
2025-05-06	Sandworm	DESKTOP-WIN10	334491	331041	3450	40358	119788	4	4
2025-05-06	Sandworm	DESKTOP-WIN11	1440558	1428548	12010	302524	757748	10	6
2025-05-06	Sandworm	SERVER-MAIL	2131339	2090898	40441	196417	546725	0	0
2025-05-06	Sandworm	SERVER-WEB	156658	153482	3176	14722	58993	0	0
2025-05-06	Sandworm	WIN-5166H0VRQLS	2336335	2288947	47388	144405	1027228	89	52
2025-05-06	Sandworm	WIN-PORTAL	349025	346029	2996	79922	150579	16	7
2025-05-07	MagicHound	DESKTOP-WIN10	454017	441432	12585	69635	168305	94	85
2025-05-07	MagicHound	DESKTOP-WIN11	1868478	1856282	12196	242851	679605	93	82
2025-05-07	MagicHound	SERVER-MAIL	2445328	2378902	66426	235608	622412	6653	244
2025-05-07	MagicHound	SERVER-WEB	132245	130799	1446	9101	46640	0	0
2025-05-07	MagicHound	WIN-5166H0VRQLS	2442697	2411915	30782	148948	1041426	211	148
2025-05-07	MagicHound	WIN-PORTAL	282291	278807	3484	40084	115525	86	57
2025-05-08	Sandworm	DESKTOP-WIN10	371791	368238	3553	34894	110741	17	6
2025-05-08	Sandworm	DESKTOP-WIN11	1745987	1734432	11555	281739	797023	10	6
2025-05-08	Sandworm	SERVER-MAIL	2032411	1994026	38385	180477	496465	3	3
2025-05-08	Sandworm	SERVER-WEB	142338	139444	2894	12841	55328	0	0
2025-05-08	Sandworm	WIN-5166H0VRQLS	2274616	2246188	28428	143170	981416	79	48
2025-05-08	Sandworm	WIN-PORTAL	469753	466231	3522	97810	178075	15	6
2025-05-09	Patchwork	DESKTOP-WIN10	430779	422592	8187	65009	194761	688	665
2025-05-09	Patchwork	DESKTOP-WIN11	1967438	1956969	10469	238373	685215	7243	873
2025-05-09	Patchwork	SERVER-MAIL	2668507	2601040	67467	228869	623551	0	0
2025-05-09	Patchwork	SERVER-WEB	170061	167127	2934	13573	56522	0	0
2025-05-09	Patchwork	WIN-5166H0VRQLS	2887597	2833955	53642	171551	1230322	0	0
2025-05-09	Patchwork	WIN-PORTAL	295596	288631	6965	31316	121608	0	0
2025-05-10	MagicHound	DESKTOP-WIN10	596528	589315	7213	69340	178271	94	85
2025-05-10	MagicHound	DESKTOP-WIN11	1748051	1732668	15383	243597	748710	104	97
2025-05-10	MagicHound	SERVER-MAIL	2201911	2157850	44061	223746	576017	6614	222
2025-05-10	MagicHound	SERVER-WEB	147408	144030	3378	16486	56380	0	0
2025-05-10	MagicHound	WIN-5166H0VRQLS	2339909	2298569	41340	147115	969643	123	87
2025-05-10	MagicHound	WIN-PORTAL	290740	287389	3351	41411	123520	86	57
2025-05-11	Benign	DESKTOP-WIN10	321413	314425	6988	40052	137546	0	0
2025-05-11	Benign	DESKTOP-WIN11	1834881	1821383	13498	246284	784954	0	0
2025-05-11	Benign	SERVER-MAIL	2415200	2369545	45655	219868	593625	0	0
2025-05-11	Benign	SERVER-WEB	251735	247934	3801	32609	97071	0	0

Continued on next page

Day	APT Group	Machine	#Events	Used	Skipped	Nodes	Edges	Mal nodes	Whitelisted
2025-05-11	Benign	WIN-5166H0VRQLS	2816722	2781915	34807	172670	1212177	0	0
2025-05-11	Benign	WIN-PORTAL	348250	343632	4618	38037	136439	0	0
2025-05-12	MagicHound	DESKTOP-WIN10	474023	471067	2956	64856	152411	86	78
2025-05-12	MagicHound	DESKTOP-WIN11	1663128	1656866	6262	186617	589639	85	75
2025-05-12	MagicHound	SERVER-MAIL	3857414	3832135	25279	408379	1179451	6615	214
2025-05-12	MagicHound	SERVER-WEB	271058	262462	8596	58328	151947	0	0
2025-05-12	MagicHound	WIN-5166H0VRQLS	2090019	2062181	27838	136163	897994	114	80
2025-05-12	MagicHound	WIN-PORTAL	232864	230194	2670	29332	89311	86	58
2025-05-13	APT29	DESKTOP-WIN10	350400	346507	3893	56721	139497	3	3
2025-05-13	APT29	DESKTOP-WIN11	1567200	1550456	16744	231808	600955	0	0
2025-05-13	APT29	SERVER-MAIL	1852814	1817974	34840	163524	451306	747	119
2025-05-13	APT29	SERVER-WEB	110893	109965	928	15032	44127	29	20
2025-05-13	APT29	WIN-5166H0VRQLS	2070843	2044682	26161	132802	903078	103	73
2025-05-13	APT29	WIN-PORTAL	254753	249251	5502	25300	97884	0	0
2025-05-14	APT29	DESKTOP-WIN10	425829	421476	4353	64342	184378	0	0
2025-05-14	APT29	DESKTOP-WIN11	9113660	9038369	75291	3060945	4277409	0	0
2025-05-14	APT29	SERVER-MAIL	2581707	2542872	38835	673664	1017120	1052	129
2025-05-14	APT29	SERVER-WEB	1127480	1113092	14388	599734	742428	0	0
2025-05-14	APT29	WIN-5166H0VRQLS	2759510	2725311	34199	173242	1197216	170	93
2025-05-14	APT29	WIN-PORTAL	304890	301879	3011	30829	102306	0	0
2025-05-15	Benign	DESKTOP-WIN10	525545	517574	7971	65726	194016	0	0
2025-05-15	Benign	DESKTOP-WIN11	4761757	4721361	40396	1543220	2686693	0	0
2025-05-15	Benign	SERVER-MAIL	4845190	4774773	70417	894958	1625716	0	0
2025-05-15	Benign	SERVER-WEB	1310756	1293326	17430	642675	857380	0	0
2025-05-15	Benign	WIN-5166H0VRQLS	5379620	5320394	59226	789963	2598797	0	0
2025-05-15	Benign	WIN-PORTAL	1382922	1363493	19429	647823	888833	0	0
Total			**282,474,445**	**278,225,840**	**4,248,605**	**32,412,413**	**103,879,244**	**331,450**	**27,310**

5.2 Node Autoencoder

As introduced in Section 3.2.4 of the proposed model, the autoencoder is employed to transform the original heterogeneous feature sets into a unified latent space of 128 dimensions. Since each node type is associated with a different set of raw features, the autoencoder provides a consistent representation that can be directly consumed by the downstream GNN models. Overall, as shown in the following subsections, the model provides encodings that not only preserve the main feature information but also embed the node type implicitly into the representations it generates.

5.2.1 Reconstruction Loss

The main evaluation metric for the node feature autoencoder is the reconstruction loss, which measures how well the model can reproduce the original feature vectors from their compressed embeddings. We employ the Mean Squared Error (MSE) loss function, which computes the squared difference between the input features and their reconstructions, averaged across all nodes. This choice is appropriate because it directly penalizes deviations in feature values and provides a smooth, differentiable objective for optimization.

Node Type	Training Loss	Test Loss	Difference
bits_job	0.000538	0.000097	-0.000441
device	0.000979	0.000796	-0.000182
dll	0.000306	0.000290	-0.000017
domain	0.000383	0.000300	-0.000083
file	0.003402	0.004869	+0.001467
ip	0.000593	0.000507	-0.000086
pipe	0.000116	0.000086	-0.000029
process	0.009363	0.010895	+0.001532
registry	0.002453	0.003787	+0.001334
scheduled_task	0.000688	0.000494	-0.000194
scheduled_task_instance	0.000260	0.000253	-0.000007
Overall	**0.003569**	**0.004569**	**+0.001000**

Table 9: Reconstruction loss per node type, reported on training and test sets. Overall results indicate low reconstruction error and good generalization. Larger node types such as *file*, *process*, and *registry* show higher losses due to greater behavioral diversity.

Table 9 summarizes the reconstruction performance across different node types, reporting both training and test losses. The overall reconstruction loss remains low, with an average of 0.0036 on the training set and 0.0046 on the test set. The small gap between training and test results indicates that the autoencoder generalizes well without severe overfitting.

Among the node types, the dominant categories such as *process* and *file* have higher reconstruction losses compared to smaller classes. This is expected, as these node types exhibit more diverse behaviors and feature patterns, making them harder to reconstruct perfectly. By contrast, smaller node types such as *dll*, *pipe*, and *scheduled_task_instance* achieve nearly identical training and test losses, reflecting stable and accurate encoding.

Overall, these results confirm that the autoencoder provides compact and robust representations of the node features. The reconstructions are sufficiently accurate across both frequent and rare node types, which is essential for supporting the downstream detection and attribution modules.

5.2.2 Sampling Strategy

We study how the mini-batch sampler affects the optimization of the node feature autoencoder. The architecture, optimizer, and learning rate schedule are kept identical across runs to isolate the sampling effect. We report reconstruction loss on the training and validation sets per epoch.

Figure 40 (left) shows the curves when using a stratified sampler that preserves the class proportion of nodes in each mini-batch. The loss drops rapidly during the first 10 epochs, followed by a slower decrease and stabilization after epoch 50. The training curve sits slightly below the validation curve most of the time, which indicates mild overfitting, but the gap is small and not consistently present. There are epochs where the training curve approaches the validation curve, which suggests that the model does not overfit aggressively and generalizes reasonably well.

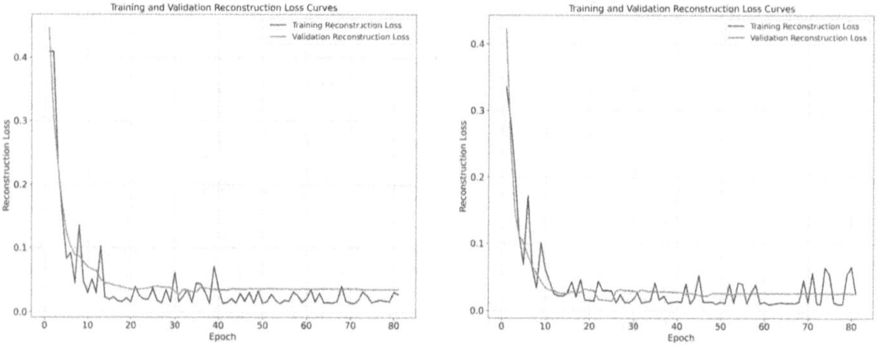

Figure 40: Training and validation reconstruction loss for the node autoencoder. Left: stratified sampler. Right: random sampler. The model stabilizes after epoch 50 with stratified sampling, and the train–validation gap remains small. Random sampling introduces large training loss variance due to non-uniform batches across epochs.

Figure 40 (right) shows the curves when using a random sampler that draws batches without any control on class or node type proportions. In this setting the training reconstruction loss is not stable. The variance is high across epochs, and occasional spikes appear even after the early fast descent. This instability arises because each epoch can receive batches from very different and non-uniform node distributions, which changes the feature distribution seen by the model and leads to inconsistent gradient updates. The validation curve remains smoother than the training curve since the validation set is fixed, which further highlights that the instability is driven by batch composition during training.

The autoencoder consistently stabilizes after 50 epochs. Stratified sampling yields smoother optimization and a small, mostly stable train–validation gap. Random sampling leads to high training variance due to non-uniform batches. For the remainder of the thesis we therefore use the stratified sampler for autoencoder training.

We further analyze the reconstruction loss broken down by node type. Figure 41 compares the validation reconstruction curves for each node type under stratified and random sampling.

In the stratified setting (left), all node types are consistently considered by the model. Even node types with relatively few instances in the dataset, such as *bits_job* and *device*, show stable learning dynamics. The dominant node types such as *file* and *process* also converge smoothly, and the overall training remains balanced across types. Importantly, the curves are smooth and stable, reflecting the fact that each epoch receives batches with a similar distribution of node types.

In contrast, random sampling (right) causes underrepresented node types such as *bits_job* and *device* to be sacrificed for dominant classes with large numbers of samples, such as *file* and *process*. Their curves plateau at higher reconstruction errors and display irregular behavior, which indicates that the model does not receive enough updates for those rare classes. The instability is again more evident in the training dynamics, with spikes and noisy convergence for certain types.

Overall, stratified sampling not only stabilizes the global loss curves but also ensures fairer treatment of all

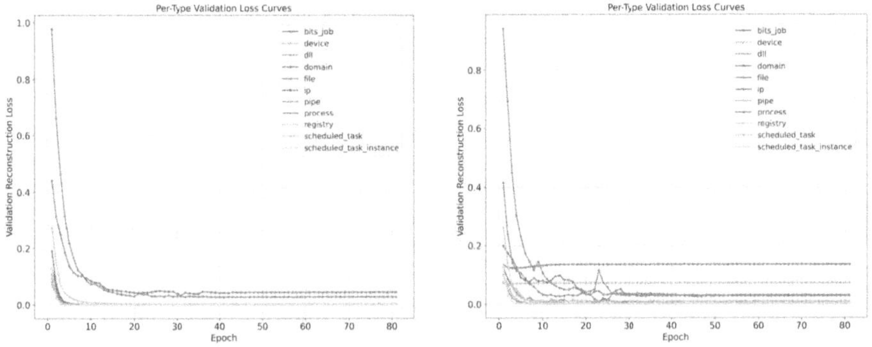

Figure 41: Per-type validation reconstruction loss curves. Left: stratified sampling ensures balanced training across all node types, including underrepresented ones such as *bits_job* and *device*. Right: random sampling sacrifices rare types and produces noisier convergence, favoring dominant classes like *file* and *process*.

node types, whereas random sampling introduces imbalance that disproportionately hurts rare node types.

5.2.3 Node Type Distinction in Encodings

Beyond reconstruction error, it is important to assess whether the autoencoder captures meaningful structural and semantic patterns in the node representations. Figure 42 shows a t-SNE visualization of the learned embeddings for nearly 98k nodes across all 11 node types.

The visualization demonstrates that the model is not only minimizing reconstruction loss but also organizing the embeddings in a way that separates different node types. Clusters corresponding to *process*, *file*, *registry*, and other types are clearly visible, with limited overlap across categories. This suggests that the autoencoder implicitly learns type-aware features, even though the node type label was not explicitly provided as an input to the model.

This property is crucial for our downstream tasks. The original provenance graph is heterogeneous and each node belongs to a specific type. To unify the representation for GNN models, we deliberately remove the explicit node type and rely only on feature vectors. However, the autoencoder encodings preserve enough information to still distinguish node types implicitly. This ensures that GNN layers, especially the attention mechanism in GAT, can leverage the inherent differences between node types without having explicit type labels in the graph structure.

5.3 Malicious Node Detection

To evaluate the performance of the malicious node detection model, we apply the trained GNN to the entire dataset and report multiple metrics that capture both detection capability and error rates. In addition to overall accuracy, we focus on metrics that are more suitable for highly imbalanced datasets such as APT provenance graphs, where benign nodes significantly dominate.

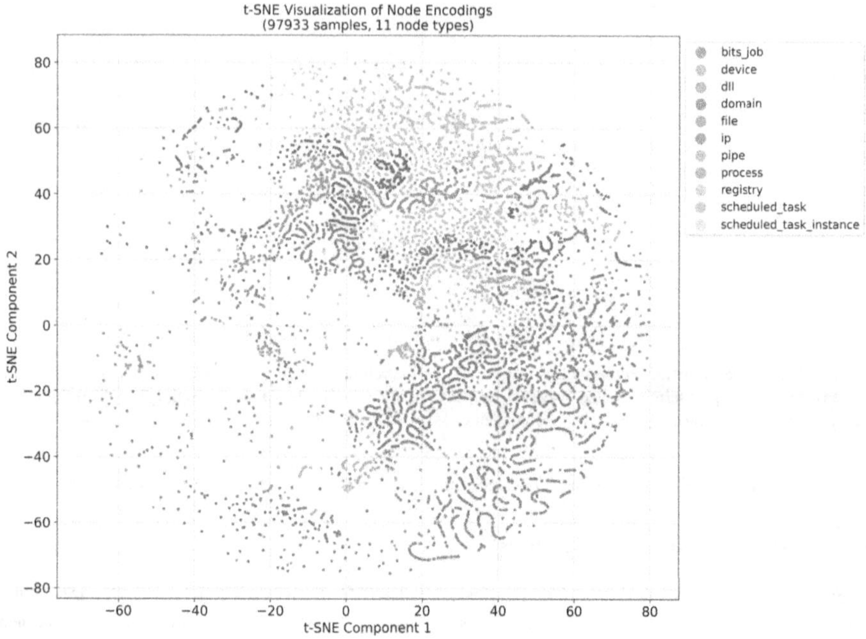

Figure 42: t-SNE visualization of the node embeddings learned by the autoencoder. Each color corresponds to a node type. The clear separation across types shows that the model encodes type-related distinctions even though node types are not explicitly provided in the input to the GNN.

Before reporting the evaluation results, it is necessary to determine an appropriate threshold for the prediction probabilities. To do this, we evaluated the trained model on a portion of the training set and plotted the Matthews Correlation Coefficient (MCC) and F1-score across different thresholds. MCC is particularly suitable for imbalanced datasets because it considers true positives, true negatives, false positives, and false negatives in a single correlation-based measure, avoiding the bias of metrics such as accuracy. As shown in Figure 43, both MCC and F1-score peak around a threshold of 0.73, which we select as the operating point for all subsequent evaluations.

Balanced accuracy is used as the primary measure. Unlike standard accuracy, it averages recall (true positive rate) and specificity (true negative rate), ensuring that both the malicious and benign classes are weighted equally. This avoids inflated results due to the overwhelming majority of benign nodes.

Recall (True Positive Rate) measures the ability of the model to correctly detect malicious nodes within each APT group. High recall is critical for minimizing missed detections, which are costly in real-world attack scenarios.

Specificity (True Negative Rate) reflects how well the model avoids false alarms by correctly classifying benign nodes. This is complemented by the **False Positive Rate (FPR)** and **False Negative Rate (FNR)**,

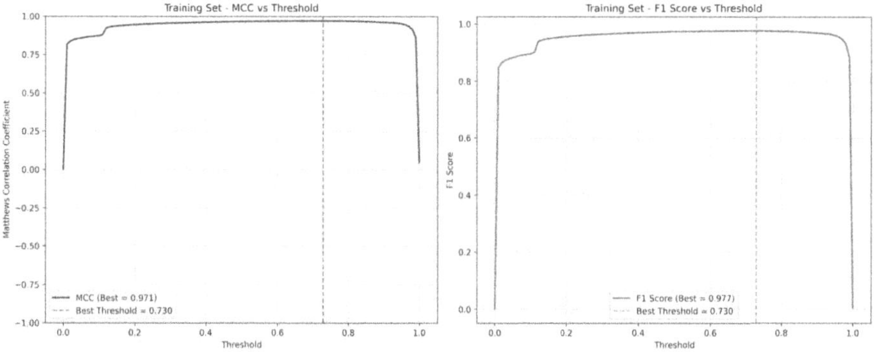

Figure 43: Threshold selection based on MCC and F1-score curves evaluated on a subset of the training set. MCC is especially suitable for imbalanced datasets, as it accounts for all four entries of the confusion matrix. The optimal threshold is 0.73, which maximizes both MCC and F1 performance.

which indicate the fraction of benign nodes incorrectly flagged as malicious, and malicious nodes missed by the detector, respectively. Together, these metrics provide a more nuanced picture of detection effectiveness. Table 10 presents the results for each APT group, the benign class, and the overall evaluation. The model achieves consistently high balanced accuracy across most APT groups, with values above 0.95 for groups such as FIN7 (0.991), Patchwork (0.981), and MagicHound (0.987). These groups also show high recall and specificity, confirming that the model is both sensitive to malicious behavior and robust against false alarms. APT29 and Sandworm show slightly lower balanced accuracy (0.968 and 0.953, respectively) due to reduced recall, indicating that some malicious nodes were missed. APT37 is the most challenging group, with a balanced accuracy of 0.916 and a recall of only 0.841, suggesting that its activity patterns overlap more with benign behavior or other APTs, making detection harder. Nevertheless, the specificity for all groups remains above 0.98, meaning false positives are rare.

The benign class is a special case. Since the true labels of all nodes in benign graphs are negative, recall and FNR are not informative in this context. The relevant metric here is the false positive rate. Although specificity is high (0.996), it is not equal to 1, which means the model still produces a small number of false alarms even on completely benign graphs. This is acceptable, because the nodes flagged as malicious are later passed into the APT classifier component, which can correctly distinguish between purely benign graphs and graphs that contain attack-related entities.

Finally, comparing the last two rows of the table provides additional insight. The *Overall* row reports metrics across all graphs, including benign ones, while the *Overall - Benign* row excludes benign recall from the balanced accuracy calculation. The slightly higher false positive rate in the *Overall - Benign* row indicates that within attack graphs, more benign nodes are falsely classified as malicious compared to the case of purely benign graphs. This shows that the model is more confident when evaluating benign graphs and is conservative in flagging nodes as malicious in the absence of attack-related entities.

Overall, the malicious node detector achieves excellent performance across the majority of APT groups, with an overall balanced accuracy of 0.983 and recall of 0.972. These results confirm that the proposed GNN-based model can reliably identify malicious nodes across diverse APT campaigns while maintaining a low false alarm rate.

Table 10: Balanced accuracy, recall, specificity, false positive rate (FPR), and false negative rate (FNR) for each APT group, benign class, and overall evaluation.

APT Group	Balanced Accuracy	Recall	Specificity	FPR	FNR
FIN7	0.990636	0.985441	0.995830	0.004170	0.014559
APT29	0.967847	0.939895	0.995799	0.004201	0.060105
APT37	0.915635	0.840757	0.990512	0.009488	0.159243
Patchwork	0.981498	0.978788	0.984208	0.015792	0.021212
Sandworm	0.952912	0.910995	0.994829	0.005171	0.089005
MagicHound	0.987174	0.982857	0.991492	0.008508	0.017143
Benign	0.498243	0.000000	0.996487	0.003513	0.000000
Overall	0.983147	0.971957	0.994338	0.005662	0.028043
Overall - Benign	0.982469	0.971957	0.992981	0.007019	0.028043

5.3.1 Evaluation Curves and Training Dynamics

To complement the threshold-based evaluation, we report threshold-free operating characteristics that are standard in the literature.

ROC curve and AUROC. Figure 44 (left) shows the ROC curve with an AUROC of 0.999. The curve closely follows the top–left corner, indicating that across thresholds the model achieves very high true positive rates while keeping false positive rates low. AUROC is threshold independent and summarizes ranking quality across the full operating range.

Precision–Recall curve and AUPRC. Figure 44 (right) shows the precision–recall curve with an AUPRC of 0.997. For imbalanced problems, PR curves are particularly informative because precision directly reflects the cost of false alarms at a given recall. The dashed horizontal line at 0.2 corresponds to the random baseline, which is determined by the sampling procedure used during training: each batch was constructed to contain 20% positive samples. The large area far above this baseline confirms strong performance in the regime that matters most for detection.

Training loss. Figure 45 shows a rapid drop in the first few epochs followed by a smooth descent and stabilization, which is consistent with the balanced accuracy and low error rates reported later.

5.3.2 Interpretability through Attention Weights

An important benefit of incorporating attention mechanisms in the final GNN layer is that the predictions of the model can be explained through the attention weights assigned to each neighbor of a target node. In the GAT formulation, attention weights are computed jointly from the features of the source and destination nodes, as well as the type of edge connecting them. This allows the model to prioritize certain interactions

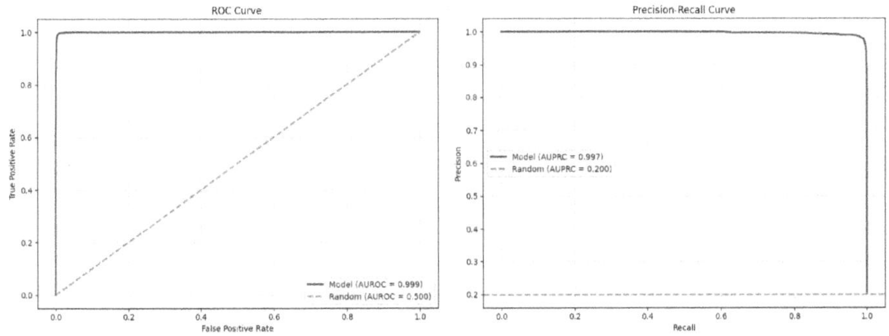

Figure 44: ROC (left) and Precision–Recall (right) curves for the malicious node detector. AUROC = 0.999 shows excellent separability, while AUPRC = 0.997 is far above the random baseline of 0.2, which reflects the 20% positive sampling ratio used per batch.

during message passing. Specifically, before aggregating neighbor features, the model computes a normalized weight for each neighbor, which reflects the relative importance of that neighbor in determining the embedding and final prediction of the target node.

To demonstrate how these weights provide interpretability, we present two case studies. Each case illustrates how the model assigns different levels of importance to specific neighbors, thereby highlighting the structural and behavioral patterns that drive malicious node classification.

5.3.2.1 Case Study 1.

Figure 46 shows a subgraph centered around the malicious process node `pro_044B914E-1148-6811-721C-0000000014C` This process corresponds to the Rokrat malware, which was spawned from the scheduled task instance `6EC272B5-6D51-44B1-993B-443F473E5A8E` (RubyLoaderTask). The attention mechanism highlights the link between the process and its parent scheduled task instance as one of the most important edges, reflecting that the model correctly identifies the provenance of the malicious behavior.

The strongest highlighted edge, however, is between the target process and its child node `6EC272B5-6D51-44B1-993B-44` which carries out the core malicious activity. This demonstrates how the model prioritizes edges that represent the main execution path of the attack. In addition, a green registry node connected to the target process is also assigned a high attention weight. This connection reflects persistence behavior, since registry modifications are commonly used by malware to maintain execution across reboots.

The heatmap in Figure 47 further confirms these observations, showing that the scheduled task instance and the registry modification receive the highest weights among all neighbors. In contrast, other benign files and processes connected to the node are given much lower weights. This highlights the ability of the GAT-based detector to focus on semantically meaningful relationships that distinguish malicious activity from normal background noise.

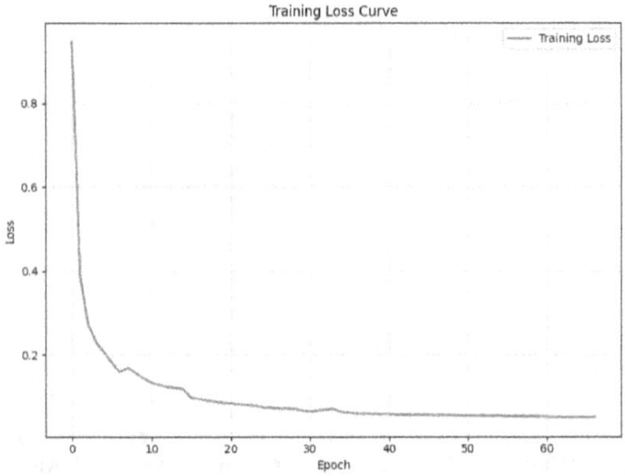

Figure 45: Training loss over epochs. The curve rapidly decreases and then stabilizes, consistent with the high operating characteristics.

5.3.2.2 Case Study 2.

Figure 48 shows a subgraph centered on the BlackMatter ransomware process `pro_EA6FB6DE-3DA6-680D-423E-`
The attention visualization highlights several neighbors that are central to the observed ransomware activity. Most notably, the file `C__Windows_Temp_sleep.exe` receives one of the highest attention weights; this binary is the payload dropped by the PowerPlant reverse shell and is responsible for executing the main malicious routine. The attention mechanism correctly prioritizes this execution path, marking it as the primary contributor to the malicious classification.

Additionally, several file and registry nodes carrying the suffix `gAUHlZUHB` are strongly highlighted in the attention heatmap. This suffix corresponds to the unique per-machine marker that BlackMatter generates and uses to identify or tag files after encryption. The high attention assigned to these nodes indicates that the model has learned to recognize the presence of these machine-specific markers as a strong signal of ransomware activity.

The subgraph also contains a subprocess `pro_EA6FB6DE-3DA7-680D-443E-000000000C00`, which the logs show executing the command:

```
bcdedit /set {current} safeboot network
```

This command modifies the Windows boot configuration to start the system in Safe Mode with Networking. This behavior, known to be used by BlackMatter and other malware families, can disable or bypass certain security protections. The attention weights show that the model emphasizes this subprocess and its related registry modifications as important cues when classifying the parent process as malicious.

Figures 48 and 49 present the network and heatmap visualizations respectively. Together they demonstrate how the GAT attention mechanism surfaces the key execution artifact (the dropped `sleep.exe`), the machine-specific file markers (`gAUHlZUHB`), and the subprocess that changes boot behavior, all of which

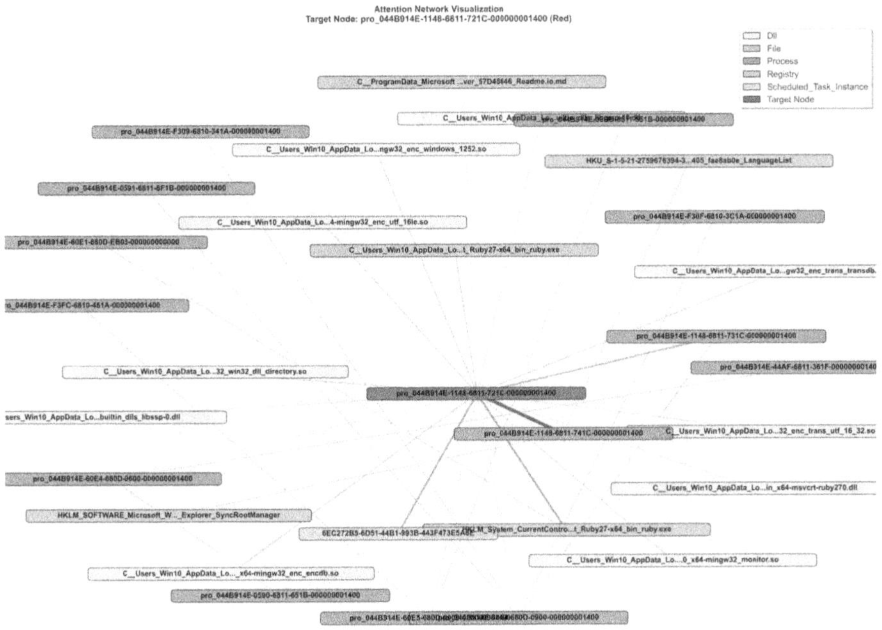

Figure 46: Attention-based subgraph visualization for Case Study 1. The target node (red) corresponds to the Rokrat malware process. The scheduled task instance (blue) and registry entry (green) are highlighted as critical neighbors by the attention mechanism.

provide an interpretable explanation for the model's detection.

5.4 APT Group Attribution

The final component of the pipeline is the APT group attribution module, which classifies the attack subgraphs into specific adversary groups. When the subgraphs are provided fully (without any node dropout), the model achieves nearly perfect accuracy, indicating that the representations learned are highly discriminative. However, such results do not reflect realistic deployment settings, since in practice some attack nodes may not yet be observed (due to partial execution of the attack) or may not be detected by the malicious node detector. Therefore, the key objective of this evaluation is to assess the robustness of the attribution model under incomplete input conditions.

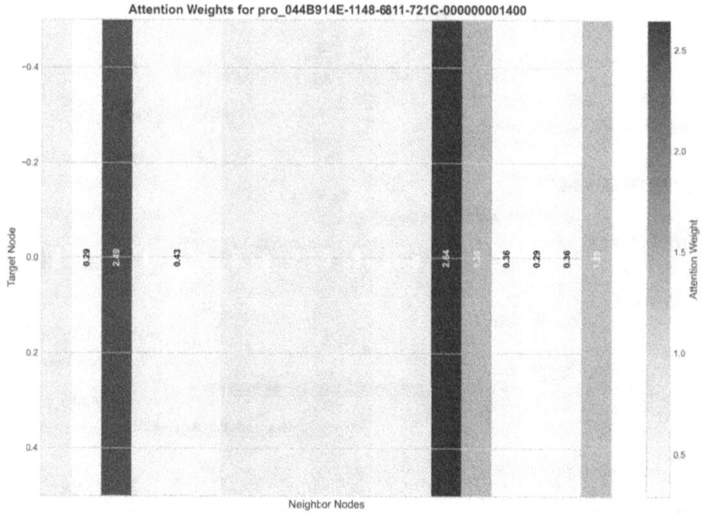

Figure 47: Heatmap of attention weights for Case Study 1. The scheduled task instance and registry entry receive the highest weights, reflecting their importance in the malicious classification.

5.4.1 Subgraph Extraction

Before performing attribution, the provenance graphs must be reduced to manageable subgraphs that preserve the malicious context while discarding unrelated background activity. This reduction is achieved through the malicious node detection module, which identifies candidate malicious nodes, and the subsequent bridge node selection, which includes key neighbors that connect the malicious nodes to the rest of the graph. The resulting subgraphs capture the relevant execution paths that drive the attribution task.

Table 11 summarizes the statistics of the extracted subgraphs across several attack and benign instances. For each case, the number of malicious nodes and bridge nodes are reported alongside the total number of nodes and edges in the reduced subgraph, together with the reduction percentage relative to the original provenance graph. Across different APT instances, the reduction percentages indicate that the resulting subgraphs are much smaller than the original graphs while still preserving sufficient context for attribution. For benign graphs, the reductions are slightly lower, which is consistent with the absence of concentrated malicious activity.

The last row aggregates the results across all experiments. In total, 144,762 malicious nodes and 6,811 bridge nodes were identified, resulting in subgraphs containing 1.57 million nodes and 13.18 million edges. Compared to the original provenance graphs, which contain 32.4 million nodes, this corresponds to an overall reduction of 4.86%. This demonstrates that the extracted subgraphs are a tiny fraction of the full dataset yet remain sufficient to retain all critical malicious behavior for reliable group attribution.

Figure 48: Attention-based subgraph for Case Study 2 (BlackMatter). The target node (red) is the ransomware process. The dropped payload (`sleep.exe`) and registry/file markers with the `gAUHlZUHB` suffix are highlighted by attention.

Table 11: Statistics of the extracted subgraphs after malicious node detection and bridge node selection. The table reports the number of malicious and bridge nodes, total nodes and edges in the reduced subgraph, and the reduction percentage relative to the original provenance graphs.

Date	APT	Host	Malicious	Bridge	Nodes	Edges	Reduction%
2025-04-09	FIN7	SERVER-MAIL	1080	9	9510	80129	5.2
2025-04-16	FIN7	SERVER-MAIL	1722	57	20934	123081	4.6
2025-04-26	FIN7	SERVER-MAIL	1386	48	16735	92674	8.7
2025-05-02	FIN7	SERVER-MAIL	1296	82	16145	84784	7.1
2025-04-10	APT29	DESKTOP-WIN10	369	63	7894	18714	36.5
2025-04-10	APT29	DESKTOP-WIN11	481	84	9201	93866	4.6
2025-04-10	APT29	SERVER-MAIL	842	11	14867	88995	9.6
2025-04-22	APT29	DESKTOP-WIN10	578	51	9857	63226	36.3
2025-04-22	APT29	DESKTOP-WIN11	1217	56	15230	164615	8.9
2025-04-22	APT29	SERVER-MAIL	737	6	9216	62429	4.7
2025-04-22	APT29	WIN-5166H0VRQLS	471	57	2903	40667	1.9

Continued on next page

Date	APT	Host	Malicious	Bridge	Nodes	Edges	Reduction%
2025-04-28	APT29	DESKTOP-WIN11	643	100	6766	93611	4.2
2025-04-28	APT29	SERVER-MAIL	752	68	11307	65341	5.6
2025-04-28	APT29	WIN-5166H0VRQLS	317	67	2614	31534	2.1
2025-05-03	APT29	DESKTOP-WIN11	617	100	7150	93419	5
2025-05-03	APT29	SERVER-MAIL	945	46	16374	86567	8.2
2025-05-03	APT29	SERVER-WEB	492	12	5741	27295	32.4
2025-05-03	APT29	WIN-5166H0VRQLS	389	67	2945	48431	2.1
2025-05-13	APT29	DESKTOP-WIN10	602	37	14493	68895	25.6
2025-05-13	APT29	SERVER-MAIL	1050	47	12868	75546	7.9
2025-05-13	APT29	SERVER-WEB	386	28	2950	18813	19.6
2025-05-13	APT29	WIN-5166H0VRQLS	660	53	4968	47808	3.7
2025-05-14	APT29	SERVER-MAIL	1889	89	34154	156176	5.1
2025-05-14	APT29	WIN-5166H0VRQLS	762	56	5786	68098	3.3
2025-04-11	APT37	DESKTOP-WIN10	1508	100	17736	69875	19.4
2025-04-17	APT37	DESKTOP-WIN10	1411	36	17107	81252	10.1
2025-04-29	APT37	DESKTOP-WIN10	877	66	9325	43968	9.7
2025-04-30	APT37	DESKTOP-WIN10	1529	80	22299	111892	17.8
2025-04-12	Patchwork	DESKTOP-WIN11	5898	91	18144	410521	17.1
2025-04-21	Patchwork	DESKTOP-WIN11	7660	48	25235	608535	13.5
2025-04-24	Patchwork	DESKTOP-WIN11	8323	32	27572	642201	14.1
2025-05-05	Patchwork	DESKTOP-WIN11	10481	0	35275	797909	16.7
2025-05-09	Patchwork	DESKTOP-WIN10	1065	30	13921	82115	21.4
2025-05-09	Patchwork	DESKTOP-WIN11	2204	19	17366	241837	7.3
2025-04-14	Sandworm	DESKTOP-WIN10	670	58	7065	34287	33.2
2025-04-14	Sandworm	DESKTOP-WIN11	476	100	13303	94650	16.8
2025-04-14	Sandworm	SERVER-MAIL	405	6	4660	66561	2.2
2025-04-14	Sandworm	WIN-5166H0VRQLS	950	90	7004	84697	4.4
2025-04-14	Sandworm	WIN-PORTAL	251	55	3665	35866	27.8
2025-04-18	Sandworm	DESKTOP-WIN10	529	39	9348	47516	39.2
2025-04-18	Sandworm	DESKTOP-WIN11	686	64	7546	83463	4.8
2025-04-18	Sandworm	WIN-5166H0VRQLS	457	41	4835	39150	3.4
2025-04-18	Sandworm	WIN-PORTAL	309	51	4932	51966	10.3
2025-04-23	Sandworm	DESKTOP-WIN10	420	53	8101	28309	25.2
2025-04-23	Sandworm	DESKTOP-WIN11	925	72	11112	95113	5.8
2025-04-23	Sandworm	WIN-5166H0VRQLS	1297	27	9589	115101	7.2
2025-04-23	Sandworm	WIN-PORTAL	334	53	4651	15653	5.9
2025-05-06	Sandworm	DESKTOP-WIN10	641	44	12124	70072	30
2025-05-06	Sandworm	DESKTOP-WIN11	1538	30	23780	235377	7.9
2025-05-06	Sandworm	WIN-5166H0VRQLS	388	62	3954	45895	2.7
2025-05-06	Sandworm	WIN-PORTAL	351	44	6085	48327	7.6
2025-05-08	Sandworm	DESKTOP-WIN10	591	73	13770	67806	39.5
2025-05-08	Sandworm	DESKTOP-WIN11	991	18	13259	128005	4.7
2025-05-08	Sandworm	SERVER-MAIL	648	62	15164	68841	8.4
2025-05-08	Sandworm	WIN-5166H0VRQLS	597	44	6228	44427	4.4
2025-05-08	Sandworm	WIN-PORTAL	444	45	7360	38433	7.5

Continued on next page

Date	APT	Host	Malicious	Bridge	Nodes	Edges	Reduction%
2025-04-15	MagicHound	DESKTOP-WIN10	786	100	13429	58966	32.2
2025-04-15	MagicHound	DESKTOP-WIN11	1949	61	23659	234633	9.8
2025-04-15	MagicHound	SERVER-MAIL	1178	65	13117	95977	6.8
2025-04-15	MagicHound	SERVER-WEB	944	68	10363	43199	41.5
2025-04-15	MagicHound	WIN-5166H0VRQLS	4840	100	15289	226041	12.5
2025-04-19	MagicHound	DESKTOP-WIN10	1240	63	17953	85061	31.8
2025-04-19	MagicHound	DESKTOP-WIN11	1246	82	15015	151884	8.4
2025-04-19	MagicHound	SERVER-MAIL	1570	10	15001	91603	8
2025-04-19	MagicHound	WIN-PORTAL	1044	57	12321	75694	46.7
2025-04-25	MagicHound	DESKTOP-WIN10	1096	32	20517	94733	30.3
2025-04-25	MagicHound	DESKTOP-WIN11	950	100	12452	138526	6.6
2025-04-25	MagicHound	SERVER-MAIL	1310	40	15060	81757	6.7
2025-05-01	MagicHound	DESKTOP-WIN10	1146	85	23121	104309	35.6
2025-05-01	MagicHound	DESKTOP-WIN11	1351	100	17459	163584	8.5
2025-05-01	MagicHound	SERVER-MAIL	1446	46	17166	86823	6.2
2025-05-01	MagicHound	WIN-5166H0VRQLS	502	73	3692	34419	2.6
2025-05-01	MagicHound	WIN-PORTAL	689	70	9849	45584	35
2025-05-07	MagicHound	DESKTOP-WIN10	975	64	17893	80139	25.7
2025-05-07	MagicHound	DESKTOP-WIN11	1668	99	24114	195162	9.9
2025-05-07	MagicHound	SERVER-MAIL	1591	63	18726	114204	7.9
2025-05-07	MagicHound	WIN-5166H0VRQLS	820	66	5566	81161	3.7
2025-05-07	MagicHound	WIN-PORTAL	782	47	8999	54297	22.5
2025-05-10	MagicHound	DESKTOP-WIN10	1691	22	26913	100290	38.8
2025-05-10	MagicHound	DESKTOP-WIN11	2232	61	30373	293829	12.5
2025-05-10	MagicHound	SERVER-MAIL	1087	49	15716	97933	7
2025-05-10	MagicHound	WIN-5166H0VRQLS	564	65	4920	77858	3.3
2025-05-10	MagicHound	WIN-PORTAL	689	81	11566	44064	27.9
2025-05-12	MagicHound	DESKTOP-WIN10	909	61	17872	71662	27.6
2025-05-12	MagicHound	DESKTOP-WIN11	1384	38	17418	198360	9.3
2025-05-12	MagicHound	SERVER-MAIL	2986	100	33119	267370	8.1
2025-05-12	MagicHound	WIN-5166H0VRQLS	507	62	5172	61406	3.8
2025-05-12	MagicHound	WIN-PORTAL	679	39	7291	46834	24.9
2025-04-13	Benign	DESKTOP-WIN10	590	36	6420	47952	25.8
2025-04-13	Benign	DESKTOP-WIN11	806	65	10864	130445	4.9
2025-04-13	Benign	SERVER-MAIL	396	16	5932	86673	2.3
2025-04-13	Benign	SERVER-WEB	393	80	3437	20387	45.2
2025-04-13	Benign	WIN-5166H0VRQLS	257	40	2454	17442	1.5
2025-04-13	Benign	WIN-PORTAL	305	60	5045	41427	33.6
2025-04-20	Benign	DESKTOP-WIN10	740	59	8905	52136	22.2
2025-04-20	Benign	DESKTOP-WIN11	1010	70	11414	145948	7.3
2025-04-20	Benign	SERVER-MAIL	492	22	10258	58491	4.9
2025-04-20	Benign	SERVER-WEB	445	50	5405	27105	35
2025-04-20	Benign	WIN-5166H0VRQLS	531	46	4429	51322	2.7
2025-04-20	Benign	WIN-PORTAL	419	36	6310	28940	31.5
2025-04-27	Benign	DESKTOP-WIN10	829	25	11972	78279	27.1

Continued on next page

Date	APT	Host	Malicious	Bridge	Nodes	Edges	Reduction%
2025-04-27	Benign	DESKTOP-WIN11	1069	100	11504	160488	5.3
2025-04-27	Benign	SERVER-MAIL	540	32	9705	64058	3.7
2025-04-27	Benign	SERVER-WEB	472	44	5121	42482	29.8
2025-04-27	Benign	WIN-5166H0VRQLS	465	56	3455	61422	1.7
2025-04-27	Benign	WIN-PORTAL	646	42	6185	41966	11
2025-05-04	Benign	DESKTOP-WIN10	489	16	5427	56712	22.6
2025-05-04	Benign	DESKTOP-WIN11	1020	100	8792	121035	5.3
2025-05-04	Benign	SERVER-MAIL	786	43	15039	84045	6.6
2025-05-04	Benign	SERVER-WEB	721	50	9856	54848	33.8
2025-05-04	Benign	WIN-5166H0VRQLS	618	58	5135	76781	2.7
2025-05-04	Benign	WIN-PORTAL	341	32	4908	42674	29.1
2025-05-11	Benign	DESKTOP-WIN10	580	40	12277	64206	30.7
2025-05-11	Benign	DESKTOP-WIN11	1150	100	17331	174141	7
2025-05-11	Benign	SERVER-MAIL	521	30	13565	59589	6.2
2025-05-11	Benign	SERVER-WEB	597	48	5549	28615	17
2025-05-11	Benign	WIN-5166H0VRQLS	548	65	4501	50086	2.6
2025-05-11	Benign	WIN-PORTAL	621	54	8264	51165	21.7
2025-05-15	Benign	DESKTOP-WIN10	947	61	21427	104669	32.6
2025-05-15	Benign	DESKTOP-WIN11	3119	36	46247	424393	3
2025-05-15	Benign	SERVER-MAIL	1824	67	33245	192207	3.7
2025-05-15	Benign	SERVER-WEB	1545	61	27985	126307	4.4
2025-05-15	Benign	WIN-5166H0VRQLS	1198	19	17803	165440	2.3
2025-05-15	Benign	WIN-PORTAL	1344	56	24813	131153	3.8
Total			144762	6811	1574223	13186725	7.5

5.4.2 Overall Robustness to Node Dropout

Table 12 reports the overall precision, recall, and F1-score of the APT attribution model under different node dropout rates, for both the multi-class setting (distinguishing between individual APT groups) and the binary setting (attack vs benign).

With no dropout, the model achieves perfect classification across both settings, confirming that the learned subgraph representations are fully separable when complete structural and contextual information is available. Introducing a modest 10% or 20% dropout only slightly reduces performance, with F1-scores above 0.96 for multi-class classification and almost 0.99 for binary classification. This shows that the model is highly robust when only a small portion of nodes is missing, which aligns with realistic conditions where some events in the provenance graph may not be captured.

At 30% dropout, the multi-class F1-score drops to 0.92, while the binary F1-score remains strong at 0.97. This gap highlights that although distinguishing between different APT groups becomes more difficult as more nodes are removed, the model is still reliable in separating attack from benign graphs. Even at 50% dropout, the binary F1-score remains above 0.93, while the multi-class score declines to 0.83.

Only at extreme dropout levels (70%) does performance significantly degrade, especially for multi-class classification (F1 of 0.61). Still, the binary setting maintains a reasonable F1 of 0.87, suggesting that the model prioritizes identifying malicious behavior over attributing it to a specific APT group when very little

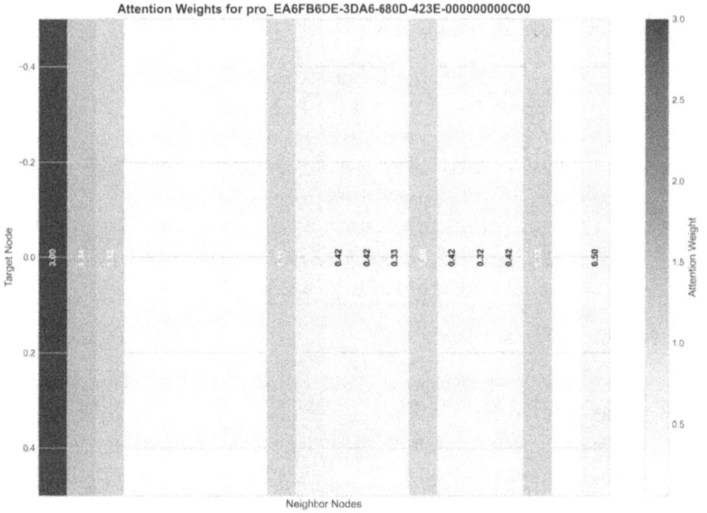

Figure 49: Heatmap of attention weights for Case Study 2. The dropped payload and the machine-unique markers receive the highest weights, indicating their importance for the malicious prediction.

evidence is available.

Overall, these results confirm that the attribution component is robust under partial information, which is essential in practice since provenance graphs collected from real systems are often incomplete.

5.4.3 Per-Class Evaluation

To better understand the effect of node dropout on specific classes, Tables 13 and 14 report precision, recall, and F1-scores for each APT group and the benign class under dropout rates of 20% and 50%.

At 20% dropout (Table 13), performance remains consistently high across all groups, with F1-scores close to or above 0.95 for most APTs. Even smaller classes, such as FIN7 and APT37, maintain strong results, suggesting that the model effectively leverages contextual relationships even when some evidence is missing. Patchwork achieves perfect scores, and benign classification remains highly accurate. These results confirm that the model is reliable when only a moderate fraction of nodes is absent.

At 50% dropout (Table 14), performance begins to vary more significantly across groups. While larger classes such as MagicHound and APT29 retain relatively high F1-scores (above 0.80), smaller classes like FIN7 are much more affected (F1 of 0.65). Interestingly, Patchwork maintains perfect recall despite a drop in precision, while Sandworm exhibits the opposite pattern with weaker precision but stronger recall. The benign class also shows some degradation but still achieves an F1 above 0.85.

Overall, this per-class analysis reveals that robustness to missing nodes is uneven: large classes and those with distinctive patterns (such as Patchwork) remain easier to classify under heavy dropout, whereas smaller

Table 12: Overall precision, recall, and F1-score of the APT attribution model across different node dropout rates for both multi-class and binary attack/benign classification.

	Multi-class Results			Attack/Benign Results		
Dropout	Prec	Rec	F1	Prec	Rec	F1
0%	1.000	1.000	1.000	1.000	1.000	1.000
10%	0.987	0.987	0.987	0.997	0.993	0.995
20%	0.969	0.969	0.969	0.988	0.990	0.989
30%	0.920	0.920	0.920	0.968	0.982	0.975
50%	0.840	0.833	0.833	0.938	0.942	0.940
70%	0.654	0.611	0.616	0.836	0.908	0.871

Table 13: Per-class results at 20% dropout

Class	Prec	Rec	F1	Support
FIN7	0.935	0.967	0.951	30
APT29	0.956	0.967	0.961	180
APT37	0.967	0.967	0.967	30
Patchwork	1.000	1.000	1.000	40
Sandworm	0.953	0.965	0.959	170
MagicHound	0.978	0.967	0.972	270
Benign	0.977	0.970	0.973	300

Table 14: Per-class results at 50% dropout

Class	Prec	Rec	F1	Support
FIN7	0.773	0.567	0.654	30
APT29	0.887	0.739	0.806	180
APT37	0.793	0.767	0.780	30
Patchwork	0.851	1.000	0.920	40
Sandworm	0.697	0.853	0.767	170
MagicHound	0.888	0.878	0.883	270
Benign	0.859	0.850	0.854	300

or less distinct classes (such as FIN7) degrade more rapidly. This underlines the importance of robustness evaluation in real-world scenarios where the provenance graph may be incomplete.

5.4.4 Confidence Evaluation

To further analyze the robustness of the APT attribution model, we evaluate the prediction *confidence* across different node dropout values. For a prediction $\hat{y}$ produced by the softmax layer over class logits $\mathbf{z}$, the confidence is defined as:

$$\text{Confidence}_{\text{multi}} = \max_{c \in C} \sigma(\mathbf{z})_c$$

where $\sigma(\mathbf{z})_c$ is the softmax probability assigned to class c, and C is the set of all APT groups and the benign class. In other words, for multiclass classification the confidence is the probability output for the predicted class.

For binary classification (attack vs. benign), confidence is defined depending on the predicted label:

$$\text{Confidence}_{\text{binary}} = \begin{cases} \sigma(\mathbf{z})_{\text{benign}}, & \hat{y} = \text{benign} \\ \sum_{c \in C_{\text{attack}}} \sigma(\mathbf{z})_c, & \hat{y} = \text{attack} \end{cases}$$

where C_{attack} denotes the set of all APT groups.

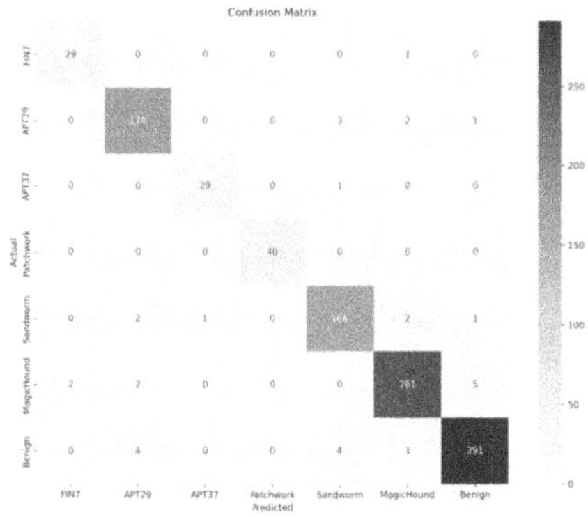

(a) Confusion matrix at 20% dropout

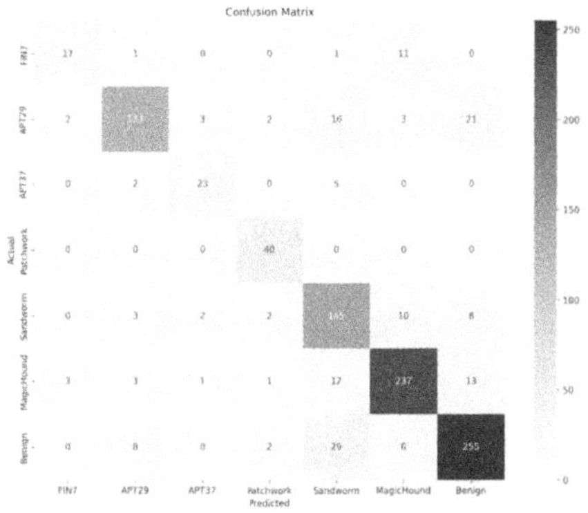

(b) Confusion matrix at 50% dropout

Figure 50: Confusion matrices at 20% and 50% dropout. At 20% dropout, most predictions remain on the diagonal with few misclassifications. At 50% dropout, off-diagonal errors increase, particularly between APT29 and Sandworm, and between MagicHound and Benign.

Apart from achieving high accuracy, it is equally important that the model is highly confident in its correct predictions, while incorrect predictions should ideally carry much lower confidence. This behavior means that when the model makes an error, it does so with hesitation, reflecting the difficulty of forcing an incorrect attribution. The resulting gap between the confidence of correct and incorrect predictions provides analysts with an interpretable signal: predictions made with unusually low confidence can be treated with caution, helping to identify potential false alarms in practice. A comprehensive confidence analysis was performed on this model using confidence histograms, as illustrated in Figure 51.

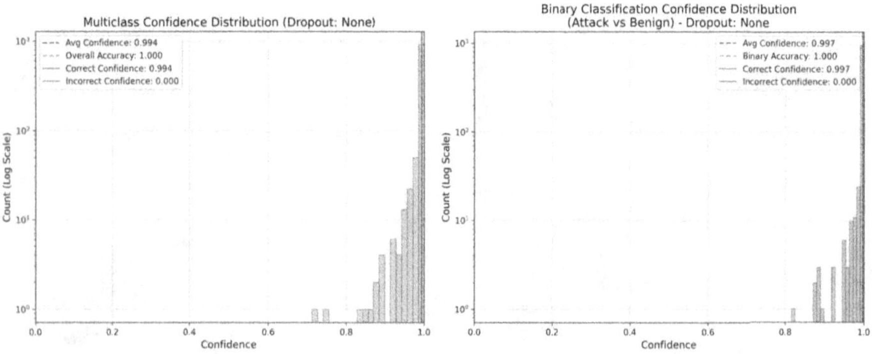

(a) Dropout: 0%

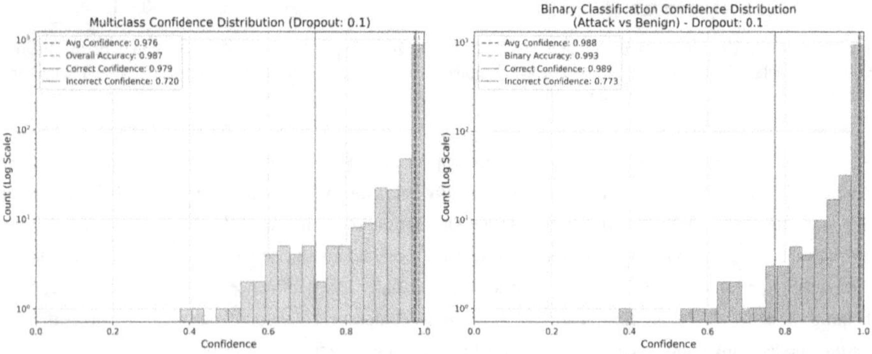

(b) Dropout: 10%

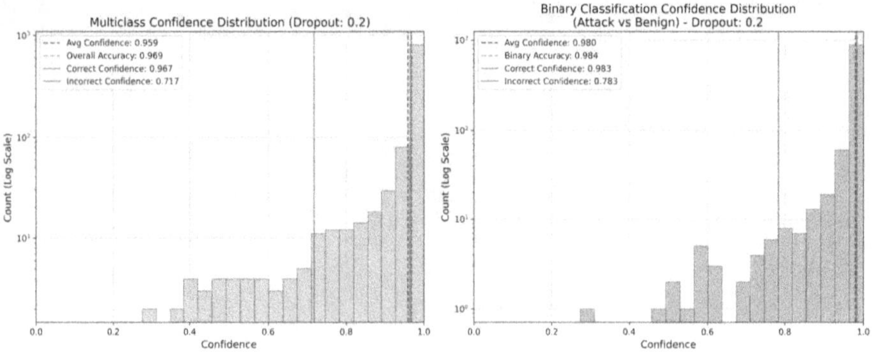

(c) Dropout: 20%

Figure 51: Confidence distributions for different node dropout values in multi-class and binary APT attribution. Each subfigure shows the distribution of prediction confidences, average confidence, and the separation between correct and incorrect predictions.

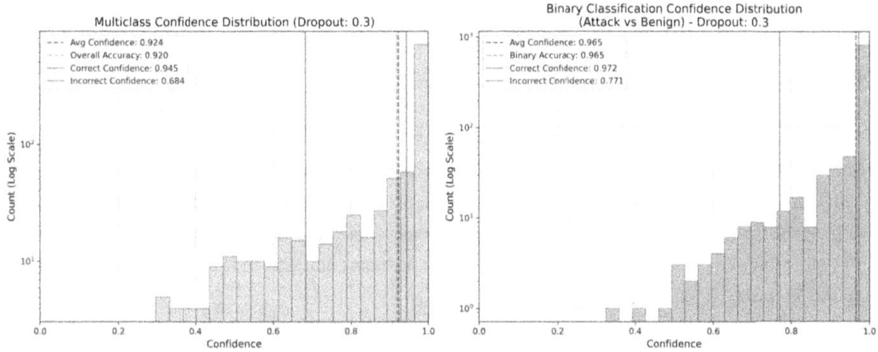

(d) Dropout: 30%

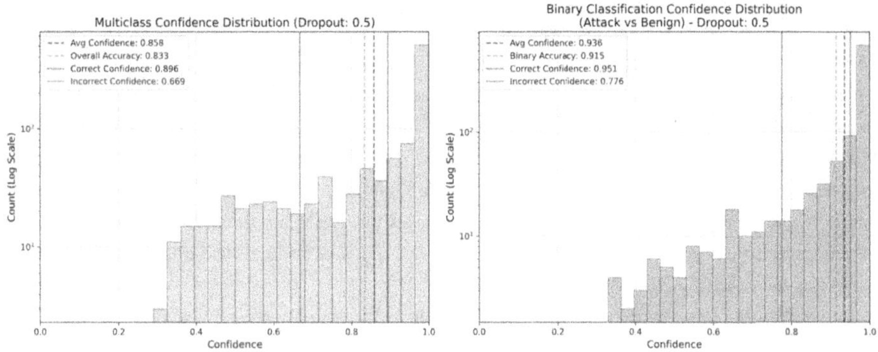

(e) Dropout: 50%

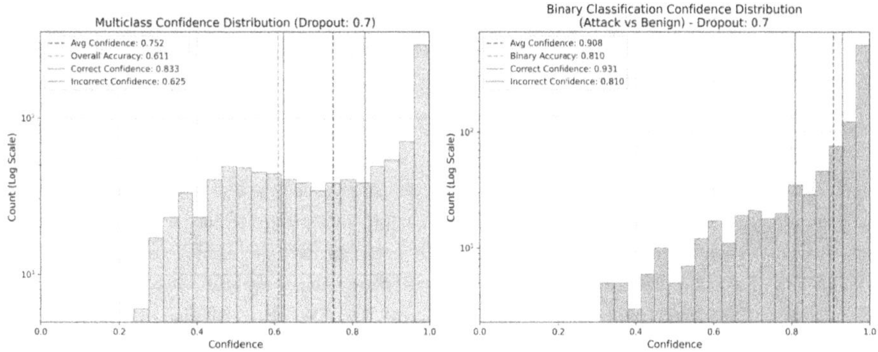

(f) Dropout: 70%

Figure 51: Confidence distributions (continued).

At **0% dropout**, both multiclass and binary classification yield perfect accuracy, with confidence values tightly clustered near 1.0. The absence of variance indicates that when the entire graph structure is available, the model produces highly certain and consistent predictions.

Introducing a small dropout of **10%** has negligible effect: average confidence remains very high (close to 0.98), and the separation between correct and incorrect predictions is maintained. This indicates that the model can tolerate minor perturbations in the graph structure without compromising certainty.

At **20% dropout**, where the model was trained, the average confidence slightly decreases (0.96 for multiclass and 0.98 for binary classification), while accuracy remains close to 97%. Incorrect predictions, although limited, exhibit substantially lower confidence (~ 0.71), demonstrating the model's ability to recognize uncertainty in misclassified cases.

Beyond this point, confidence distributions start to degrade. With **30% dropout**, the average confidence drops to 0.92 (multiclass) and 0.97 (binary), and the histograms show a more noticeable tail of lower-confidence predictions. Importantly, correct predictions still retain higher confidence compared to incorrect ones, which is a desirable calibration property.

At **50% dropout**, accuracy decreases more sharply ($\sim$ 83% multiclass, 91% binary), and the distributions widen, indicating less certainty in predictions. Nevertheless, the average confidence of correct predictions remains relatively high (~ 0.90), while incorrect predictions are markedly less confident (~ 0.67).

Finally, at the extreme case of **70% dropout**, the model struggles to maintain robustness. Multiclass accuracy falls to $\sim$ 61%, with a noticeable flattening of the confidence distribution, while binary classification retains higher robustness ($\sim$ 81% accuracy). This suggests that the binary formulation is more resilient to missing information, as the model still detects whether a graph is attack-related even when fine-grained attribution to a specific APT group becomes unreliable.

In summary, the confidence evaluation shows that the model is not only accurate but also well-calibrated. Correct predictions consistently appear with high confidence, while noticeably lower confidence values accompany incorrect predictions. This separation provides a useful interpretability signal: analysts can treat low-confidence predictions as potential false alarms and prioritize high-confidence cases for attribution. The ability to convey such uncertainty is essential in real-world threat hunting, where decisions must be made under incomplete or noisy evidence.

5.5 Comparative Analysis

To place the proposed model in context, we conduct a comparative analysis against prior approaches from the literature. Two representative models were selected and re-implemented to operate on the APT dataset introduced in Section 4. The first baseline is **ATLAS** [51], one of the most well-known works in this domain, which follows a sequence-based learning approach derived from provenance graphs. We chose ATLAS as the representative of sequence-based models such as LogShield [17]. The second baseline is **APT-MGL** [24], which follows a masked graph representation learning paradigm. We chose this model as the representative of anomaly detection methods that are trained on benign data and attempt to detect attacks through deviations from normal user behavior. Other examples in this family include KAIROS [21], ProcSAGE [22], Prov2Vec [23], and RT-APT [25].

Since these baselines were originally designed for different datasets and computational environments, we adapted their implementations to fit our provenance graph data and experimental setup. In particular, certain components of the original models were simplified to ensure compatibility with our framework and to accommodate the available computational resources, while preserving their core design principles. In the following, we describe each baseline model, the modifications made during integration, and the results of applying them to our dataset.

5.5.1 ATLAS

ATLAS [51] is a sequence-based learning framework for attack investigation from system audit logs. Its central idea is that while low-level details of attacks vary, their high-level strategies follow recurring patterns that can be learned from event sequences. By abstracting provenance graphs into compact sequences, ATLAS enables machine learning models to generalize across different APT campaigns.
The architecture of ATLAS has two main phases: *sequence model learning* and *attack investigation*. In the learning phase, raw audit logs are parsed into a causal graph of processes, files, and network connections. This graph is optimized to reduce noise, then converted into sequences that are abstracted into a small vocabulary and embedded into vectors. To address the significant class imbalance between benign and malicious sequences, ATLAS employs selective sampling that combines the undersampling of benign sequences with mutation-based oversampling of attack sequences. The resulting dataset is used to train a deep sequence model based on LSTMs, enhanced with convolutional layers and dropout for regularization.
In the investigation phase, the trained model evaluates sequences constructed around suspicious entities (e.g., IPs, processes, files). Entities classified as attack-related are linked to reconstruct the attack story, providing analysts with an interpretable timeline of malicious behavior. The evaluations they conducted on ten APT scenarios showed high effectiveness, with ATLAS achieving precision of 91.06% and recall of 97.29%.
In summary, ATLAS combines provenance graph abstraction, sequence learning, and sampling strategies to detect attack entities and automatically recover attack stories.

5.5.1.1 Our Implementation.

To adapt ATLAS to our dataset, we extended the event vocabulary beyond the three entity types used in the original work (process, file, and network connections). Our vocabulary encompasses a richer set of entities and actions, including process access, task invocation, various categories of files and processes (e.g., user, system32, programs, windows), and connection types (IP, pipe, DNS, domain). The full mapping contains 30 tokens, ranging from high-level actions like `execute`, `read`, and `write`, to entity-specific tokens such as `scheduled_task`, `bits_job`, and `pipe`. This expansion ensures that the sequences capture the heterogeneity of our provenance graphs. However, due to the very large number of `registry` and `dll` nodes in the dataset, which caused sequences to become excessively long, we excluded these categories from the vocabulary.
For sequence generation, we followed the original ATLAS algorithm but introduced constraints to cope with resource limitations. Specifically, we limited the number of malicious nodes used to generate sequences, with incremental caps depending on the number of malicious nodes included. For example, we extracted at most 1000 sequences from 2 malicious nodes, 2000 sequences from 3 nodes, 3000 sequences from 4

nodes, and 4000 sequences from 5 nodes. This controlled expansion prevented combinatorial explosion while maintaining sufficient coverage of malicious activity.

We also limited the maximum sequence length to 512 tokens. Sequences exceeding this length were split into subsequences of length 512 with a 25% overlap between adjacent subsequences to preserve contextual continuity. The final model architecture remained consistent with the original ATLAS design, consisting of embedding layers followed by LSTM units with convolutional enhancements.

For training, we used the following parameters: embedding dimension of 128, LSTM output size of 256 units, and a maximum sequence length of 512. The model was trained with a batch size of 4096 over 8 epochs, using a classification threshold of 0.5. These settings were optimized to fit our available GPU resources while ensuring stable training for large-scale sequence data.

5.5.1.2 Results and Analysis.

Figure 52 shows the training and validation loss and accuracy curves for our ATLAS implementation. Both training and validation losses decrease rapidly during the first epochs, while accuracy increases and stabilizes after around three epochs. The gap between training and validation curves remains moderate, indicating that the model generalizes reasonably well given the complexity of the data and the limited number of training epochs. Validation accuracy stabilizes around 0.85, slightly above the training accuracy of 0.80, which suggests that the model benefits from dropout and regularization in mitigating overfitting.

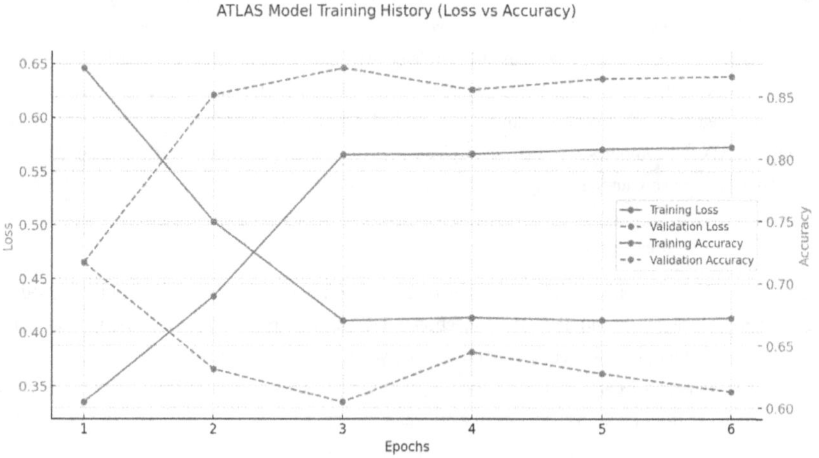

Figure 52: Training and validation loss/accuracy curves for ATLAS.

The overall evaluation metrics are summarized in Table 15. The confusion matrix shows that the model predicted 313,115 nodes as benign and 139,134 nodes as malicious, with 102,442 true positives, 20,638 false negatives, and 36,692 false positives. Overall accuracy is 0.87, with balanced performance across classes.

Table 15: ATLAS classification performance on benign vs. malicious nodes.

Class	Precision	Recall	F1-Score	Support
Benign	0.93	0.89	0.91	329169
Malicious	0.74	0.83	0.78	123080
Overall	0.88	0.87	0.88	452249

These results demonstrate that ATLAS effectively distinguishes between benign and malicious nodes, with strong precision for benign entities (0.93) and a reasonably high recall for malicious nodes (0.83). The trade-off is visible in the 36k false positives, where benign sequences are misclassified as malicious. To mitigate the effect of class imbalance (benign nodes dominate), class weights were applied in the loss function, which improved recall for malicious nodes without substantially reducing benign precision.

Table 16 provides a per-group breakdown. FIN7 and MagicHound achieve the strongest results, with F1-scores of 0.824 and 0.869, respectively. APT29 also performs well with F1 of 0.816 and very high recall (0.964), though at the cost of lower precision. By contrast, APT37 remains challenging with lower precision (0.529) and F1 of 0.631, suggesting its activity overlaps heavily with benign behavior. Patchwork achieves balanced performance (F1 of 0.737) while Sandworm lags with precision and recall both lower, resulting in F1 of 0.581. Notably, the confidence values reflect this disparity: groups like MagicHound and FIN7 show higher average confidence, while Sandworm's very low average confidence (0.135) signals instability in predictions.

Table 16: Per-APT group evaluation results for ATLAS.

APT Group	Total	Mal	Ben	Pred Mal	Pred Ben	Acc	Prec	Rec	F1	Avg Conf
APT29	39055	19338	19717	26355	12700	0.784	0.707	0.964	0.816	0.553
APT37	19535	9555	9980	14150	5385	0.553	0.529	0.783	0.631	0.576
FIN7	20525	10154	10371	13121	7404	0.801	0.731	0.945	0.824	0.538
MagicHound	95223	46370	48853	52724	42499	0.864	0.817	0.929	0.869	0.488
Patchwork	41414	20471	20943	20804	20610	0.737	0.731	0.743	0.737	0.531
Sandworm	236497	17192	219305	11980	224517	0.948	0.707	0.493	0.581	0.135

Overall, the ATLAS baseline demonstrates that sequence-based learning can achieve solid results on APT provenance data, particularly for groups with distinctive sequential behavior such as FIN7 and MagicHound. However, its limitations are clear in the uneven per-group performance, especially for Sandworm and APT37, where overlap with benign sequences reduces precision and stability. These findings highlight why graph-based approaches, such as our proposed model, are better suited for capturing structural dependencies and handling diverse APT behaviors.

5.5.2 APT-MGL

APT-MGL [24] is a provenance-based APT detection framework that leverages masked graph representation learning. Unlike supervised methods that rely on labeled attack data, APT-MGL employs a self-supervised approach, training solely on benign provenance graphs and transforming the problem into anomaly detection, which flags nodes whose behaviors deviate from the learned patterns of normal activity.

The architecture consists of four main stages. First, raw system audit logs are preprocessed into provenance graphs, where nodes represent processes, files, or network entities and edges capture causal relationships. Second, node features are collected along three complementary dimensions: node type, behavioral features (capturing interaction patterns), and degree features (capturing frequency of interactions). Word2Vec embeddings and a multi-head self-attention mechanism are used to enrich and fuse these features. Third, the fused features are passed through a masked graph self-encoder, based on GraphMAE2 and GAT layers. By randomly masking node attributes and requiring the model to reconstruct them, the encoder learns robust representations that capture both feature semantics and structural context. Finally, in the detection stage, embeddings are analyzed via unsupervised outlier detection (e.g., KNN-based), where nodes with anomalous embedding patterns are flagged as potentially malicious.

In summary, APT-MGL combines provenance graph preprocessing, multi-view node feature fusion, and self-supervised masked graph learning to build a model of benign system behavior. Malicious entities are then detected as outliers, enabling effective APT detection without requiring labeled attack data.

5.5.2.1 Our Implementation.

In adapting APT-MGL to our dataset, we made several modifications to balance fidelity to the original design with the scalability demands of our provenance graphs. Instead of using the feature fusion module proposed in the paper, we employed our own node feature autoencoder (introduced in Section 3) to unify the heterogeneous node features into a dense latent representation. This ensured consistency across components of our pipeline and reduced redundancy in feature processing.

For the graph representation learning module, we followed the architecture described in the APT-MGL paper, which is based on masked graph representation learning with GAT layers. However, due to the scale of our provenance graphs, applying this directly to the entire graph was computationally infeasible. To address this, we adopted subgraph sampling using PyTorch's `NeighborSampler` with a fanout of $(25, 25, 25)$. This strategy extracts relatively large subgraphs around each target node, capturing a broad context of interactions while keeping the sampled graphs within GPU memory limits.

To train the graph representation model, we sampled 1024 subgraphs from each graph in the training set. While each subgraph was passed individually through the model to keep computations feasible, gradients were accumulated across 256 subgraphs before performing a backward pass and updating the model parameters. This gradient accumulation strategy effectively simulates training with large batches while respecting memory constraints, enabling stable optimization over the large-scale dataset.

For the anomaly detection stage, we followed the approach described in the APT-MGL paper and fitted a K-Nearest Neighbors (KNN) model using only benign training data. The embeddings of benign nodes had an average distance of 0.1602 to their k nearest neighbors, which we used as the baseline for normal behavior. We applied $\theta = 3$ as the detection threshold, meaning that nodes with an average distance greater than 3×0.1602 were flagged as anomalous. This approach enables the model to identify malicious nodes as deviations from benign behavior, aligning with the self-supervised anomaly detection paradigm of APT-MGL.

Overall, this implementation preserves the core design of APT-MGL while adapting it to our dataset through the use of our feature autoencoder, subgraph sampling, gradient accumulation, and threshold-based outlier detection.

5.5.2.2 Results and Analysis.

Table 17 summarizes the evaluation results of our APT-MGL implementation on a balanced test set. We report precision, recall, F1-score, ROC-AUC, and anomaly rate for each APT group, as well as the aggregate performance across all groups.

Table 17: APT-MGL evaluation results per APT group on a balanced dataset.

APT Group	Precision	Recall	F1-Score	ROC-AUC	Anomaly Rate (%)
APT29	0.886	0.978	0.929	0.953	55.18
FIN7	0.856	1.000	0.923	0.979	58.40
MagicHound	0.749	1.000	0.856	0.924	66.78
APT37	0.579	1.000	0.733	0.568	86.43
Sandworm	0.632	0.782	0.699	0.671	61.88
Patchwork	0.700	0.583	0.636	0.617	41.65
All Groups	0.715	0.877	0.787	0.795	61.36

The results show that APT-MGL achieves strong recall across most groups, often close to 1.0, reflecting its anomaly-detection nature: it is highly sensitive to deviations from benign behavior. However, this comes at the cost of precision, which is lower for several groups (e.g., Sandworm at 0.632 and APT37 at 0.579), indicating a higher rate of false alarms. This trade-off is also reflected in the anomaly rate, which is elevated for some groups (e.g., APT37 with 86.4%), suggesting the model tends to over-flag nodes as anomalous in some instances.

Among the groups, FIN7 and MagicHound stand out with strong balanced performance (F1-scores above 0.85 and ROC-AUC above 0.92). By contrast, Patchwork and APT37 are more challenging: Patchwork suffers from low recall (0.583), while APT37 achieves perfect recall but very low precision, resulting in a modest F1 score of 0.733. These differences illustrate that the effectiveness of anomaly detection varies depending on how distinct the group's malicious behavior is from benign activity.

Overall, APT-MGL achieves an aggregate F1 Score of 0.787 and an ROC AUC of 0.795 across all groups. This confirms that masked graph representation learning combined with benign-only training can detect a wide range of APT activities, but at the cost of increased false positives compared to supervised approaches.

6 Conclusion

Advanced Persistent Threats (APTs) remain one of the most significant challenges in cybersecurity due to their stealthy and multi-stage nature. This thesis presented EAGLE-APT, an edge-aware provenance graph learning framework for end-to-end APT detection and attribution. The framework was developed to meet the dual goals of reliably identifying malicious activity at the node level and attributing entire campaigns to specific adversary groups, while remaining scalable and interpretable for practical use.

The research began by addressing the lack of suitable data for reproducible evaluation. A comprehensive dataset of simulated APT campaigns was created, capturing realistic adversarial strategies over multiple weeks in a controlled enterprise environment. Unlike existing datasets that are outdated or narrowly scoped, this dataset reflects modern Windows-based infrastructures and diverse adversarial tactics, and it incorporates benign background activity that makes the attack scenarios more representative of real-world conditions. This dataset provided the foundation for training, evaluation, and comparison throughout the study.

Building on this dataset, raw audit logs were transformed into heterogeneous provenance graphs that preserve the diversity of system-level interactions. Unlike prior work that limits analysis to processes, files, and network sockets, the graphs used in this work include entities such as scheduled tasks, registry keys, DLLs, and bits jobs. This richer representation ensures that the footprints of sophisticated attacks are not lost during preprocessing, allowing for the capture of subtle behaviors that are crucial for attribution.

On top of this foundation, the framework introduced a malicious node detection model based on graph neural networks. By combining GraphSAGE aggregation with edge-aware GAT layers, the model was able to capture both structural dependencies and the semantics of relation types. The evaluations demonstrated that this component consistently achieves strong performance across a wide range of APT groups. It is both sensitive to malicious activity and resistant to false alarms, with only the stealthiest groups showing noticeable drops in recall. Notably, the attention mechanism provided interpretable explanations of why specific nodes were flagged, consistently highlighting key interactions such as persistence mechanisms or command-line abuse. This interpretability strengthens the model's practical value, as analysts can better understand and validate its predictions.

From these detections, the framework constructs malicious subgraphs by expanding around flagged nodes and incorporating bridge structures. This step significantly reduces the size of the original provenance graphs, which contain tens of millions of nodes, while retaining the necessary context for higher-level attribution. The evaluation confirmed that these subgraphs preserve the critical attack paths and are both manageable for machine learning and meaningful for analysis.

The attribution module then classifies the extracted subgraphs into specific APT groups. Initial experiments with complete graphs demonstrated perfect accuracy; however, to reflect realistic deployment conditions, the focus shifted to robustness when some nodes are missing. Evaluations under increasing node dropout shown that the model maintains high accuracy even when substantial portions of the graph are unavailable. Up to moderate dropout levels, performance remains strong; however, at higher dropout rates, the system still reliably distinguishes benign graphs from attack graphs, even if precise attribution becomes more challenging. Confidence analysis added another dimension to the evaluation. Correct predictions consistently appeared with high confidence, while incorrect ones carried noticeably lower values. This separation provides analysts with a valuable measure of uncertainty, allowing them to treat low-confidence predictions with greater caution.

To contextualize the proposed framework, two baseline models from the literature were re-implemented: ATLAS, which represents sequence-based learning approaches, and APT-MGL, which represents anomaly detection models trained solely on benign data. Both baselines performed reasonably well in specific scenarios but also revealed essential limitations. ATLAS demonstrated that sequential patterns are effective for some groups but struggled with stealthier behaviors, producing uneven results across campaigns. APT-MGL was highly sensitive to anomalies, achieving strong recall, but at the expense of precision, resulting in more false positives. In contrast, EAGLE-APT demonstrated a more balanced performance across groups, combining strong detection rates with robustness and interpretability, thereby highlighting the advantages of graph-based representation learning.

In conclusion, this thesis demonstrated that provenance-based graph learning can effectively support both malicious entity detection and campaign-level attribution in realistic APT scenarios. The combination of heterogeneous graph construction, type-aware feature encoding, edge-aware GNNs, and context-preserving subgraph extraction provides a comprehensive pipeline that is accurate, robust, and interpretable. Beyond the immediate results, the dataset created for this work establishes a platform for future research in the field. While EAGLE-APT demonstrates strong performance and robustness in both detection and attribution, several directions remain for future work. First, the dataset can be extended to include additional APT groups, longer campaign timelines, and more diverse environments, such as Linux or hybrid infrastructures, further testing the model's adaptability. Second, incorporating temporal dynamics more explicitly into the graph learning process may improve the ability to capture long-term dependencies across attack stages, making attribution more resilient against stealthy behaviors. Third, more enhanced feature extraction and engineering can be explored, incorporating richer semantic signals from system behavior to strengthen node representations. Finally, implementing incremental graph generation over time, for example by using graph databases, would enable on-the-fly detection and attribution. This would move the framework closer to a real-time pipeline, bridging the gap between offline analysis and practical deployment in enterprise environments.

www.ingramcontent.com/pod-product-compliance
Lightning Source LLC
La Vergne TN
LVHW010732061126
851857LV00014B/1445